# The Formula for Accelerated Change

$$V_X P^2{}_X A_X T = C_{©}$$

*"Visionary People 2gether in Action over Time make Change"*

## How to Become a Visionary Leader, achieve Success and Sustainable Development

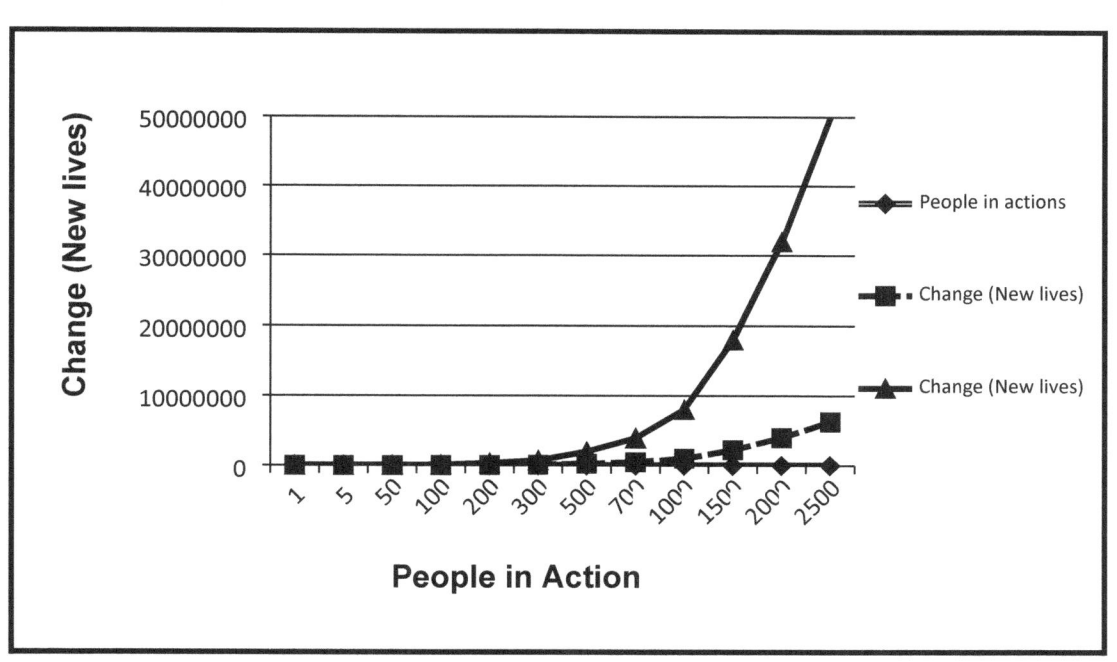

# Juvenal Turatsinze

This book *The Formula for Accelerated Change* is dedicated to African Youth who are called to transform Africa into a continent of opportunities, prosperity and peace.

*"It always seems impossible until it's done."* Nelson Mandela

Juvenal TURATINZE

# CONTENT

# The Formula for Accelerated Change

# PREFACE

Change is a permanent fact of life. Human beings always want change. We want positive change that improves our lives and leads to new and better lives. We want to become successful. When we wake up in the morning we think and plan about what we are going to do during the day to make change for ourselves or for others. Most people want to change the world for the better. However, despite our desire to make change, most of the time we find it difficult to make the change we want.

Change is natural and will happen whether we want it or not. When a change happens in our favour, it is fine and we are happy; but when it is a change that we don't want, it is a problem and we resist it. The key problem in our lives is how to make the change we want, or turn the change we do not want in our favour.

This book gives you a scientific approach to making the changes you desire or managing change in your favour when it happens. For the first time you have a holistic formula for change. This formula for change has all the key factors of change; and it builds relationships between them to produce change. The factors of change are: vision, people, actions and time. Each factor is organic in nature, because it grows with time when nourished with the right ingredients.

You are going to learn how to develop these factors and ingredients and how to combine them to make the change you desire. These factors and ingredients are multipurpose; they can allow you to make the change you want at all levels and in different fields, whether personal or social, political, economic, technological, and cultural, etc.

The result of the combination of these factors in the formula will make you think differently, change your mindset and produce paradigm shifts. You are going to realise that you are born to be a leader with the purpose of making a change on earth. You are going to discover that you can make any change you want in the world if you can build a critical mass of people with a common vision. You will understand the power of vision to dismantle the status quo, to overrun the minds of the majority and find out how it creates a new identity that crosses all borders and cultures.

This book is meant for those who want to make change in their area of interests or calling. First, it will help you to achieve personal change so that you can influence others to change or change the environment you are in.

Juvenal TURATINZE

**The Formula for Accelerated Change**

As the author of this book, I am on the same journey of changing myself, improving myself to become able to serve others with my talents. My personal vision is the advent of a world without poverty where every human being is able to use their potential to meet all their needs and serve others with their God-given gifts for the common good.

Juvenal TURATSINZE

# I. INTRODUCTION

You are seeking positive changes in your life and in the environment you live in. Like other people, you want positive changes in all dimensions of your life, be it physical, mental, emotional, spiritual, economic, social, political, cultural or environmental. However, even if you know or feel the change you want in your life and in society or in the environment you live in, you may not know how to achieve it.

This book will help you discover how you can make the change you want in your life or in the society you live in. It gives you a simple formula for change and explains how it can be used. This scientific approach to understanding change makes it easier for you to plan and make the change you desire and to manage it when it happens.

The Formula for Accelerated Change reveals the key factors of change and shows how they are related and combined to produce and manage change. Every factor is explained in detail so that you can understand it fully and to help you understand how it contributes to making change.

For change to happen, the following four factors are necessary: **vision**, **people**, **action** and **time**. Each factor has a multiplier effect on change. That is why if one is missing, the change does not happen, so the change becomes null.

- Where there is no vision (vision=0), there is no change (change=0). Change starts only with a vision of a new image of how things should be.
- Without people (people=0), no change (change=0). Change happens by people, with people and for people.
- Without actions (actions=0), no change (change=0). Change cannot happen if nothing is done.
- If time is zero (time=0), change is zero (change=0). All changes need time, and change comes with time.

### The Formula for Accelerated Change

The Formula for Accelerated Change is developed as follows:

---

**Vision x People² x Action x Time = Change**

$$V \times P^2 \times A \times T = C$$

**'Visionary People Together in Action over Time make Change (New lives)'**

---

Once you understand this formula and work on the factors within the formula, then you can begin to make the change you desire to achieve the results you want.

Any change starts with a vision generated by a person called a visionary leader or initiator. When the created vision concerns other people, the initiator should share his vision with the people concerned and mobilise them to take collective actions. Actions need time to plan, implement and have impact. When people are committed to one vision, synergy is created and this produces an exponential effect on people leading to the vision and intended change being achieved.

Synergy[1] is what happens when one plus one equals four, ten or a hundred or even a thousand. The result is overwhelming when two or more respectful human beings determine to go beyond their preconceived and individual ideas to meet a great challenge and achieve a common vision.

This book focuses on the change made in improving the lives of people. It is about creating new lives where people are fulfilled in all dimensions of their life, and enjoy it to the full.

---

[1] Synergy is defined by Steven Covey in *The 7 habits of the most effective people*.

# II. BACKGROUND

The development of the formula for change is not new. A formula for change was created by David Gleicher while he was working with Arthur D. Little in the early 1960s, and refined by Kathie Dannemiller in the 1980s. Their formula provides a model to assess the relative strengths affecting the likely success of organisational change programmes.

The original formula, as created by Gleicher and published by Beckhard,[2] is: $C = (ABD) > X$, where $C$ is change, $A$ is the status quo dissatisfaction, $B$ is the desired clear state, $D$ is the practical steps to the desired state, and $X$ is the cost of the change. Richard Beckhard and Rubin Harris first published their change equation in 1977 in *Organizational Transitions: Managing Complex Change*.

Dannemiller[3] coined the term, '**Formula for Change**' which is sometimes called *Gleicher's Formula*. Dannemiller's version of the formula **is: $D \times V \times F > R$,** where **D** is Dissatisfaction with how things are now; **V** is the Vision of what is possible; **F** is First, the concrete steps that can be taken towards the vision; and **R** is Resistance.

There must be three factors present for meaningful organisational change to take place. If the product of these three factors is greater than the Resistance, then change is possible. Because D, V, and F are multiplied, if any one is absent (zero) or low, then the product will be zero or low and therefore not capable of overcoming the resistance.

From the point of view of new analysis, the formulas for change proposed above by Beckhard, Gleicher and Dannemiller are seen as simplistic and they do not say everything about change. Their analysis of change was limited to organisations. The new critical analysis proves that the factors of **dissatisfaction** and **resistance** are not relevant in the formula for change as explained below.

**Dissatisfaction**

In these old formulas, it is assumed that change can happen only when people are dissatisfied. But the question we can raise here is to know why and when people are satisfied or dissatisfied.

The reality is that people are satisfied (or not dissatisfied) when they lack knowledge or information about a better alternative. Dissatisfaction is caused by the lack of knowledge or the absence of vision of how things should be. Dissatisfaction is an automatic result of new knowledge and vision. For example, you do not need something when you don't know if it exists or you won't desire a situation

---

[2] Beckhard, R.,(1969), *Organization Development: Strategies and Models*, Addison-Wesley, Reading, MA.

[3] Dannemiller, K. D., and Jacobs, R. W., (1992), 'Changing the way organizations change: A revolution of common sense', *The Journal Of Applied Behavioral Science*, 28(4), pp.480-498.

you are not aware of. Many people were satisfied with the iPhone 3 or 4 until the iPhone 5 and 6 came along. When it came with its new functions and more capacity, they became dissatisfied with the former. Dissatisfaction in people is created by new knowledge and information on how the new product can make their lives much easier.

Every situation can be improved. People always look for the better as they do not want to settle for the bad or the good only. The main problem is that they often lack the knowledge of a better situation. Dissatisfaction is a result of new thoughts caused by the acquisition of new knowledge or information. Change is created only from new thoughts and driven by a new vision. Dissatisfaction can always be created by providing new knowledge, information or an alternative to the status quo. New knowledge and a new vision automatically make the status quo obsolete, and this inevitably ignites the will of change.

## Vision

Vision is a key factor of change. A vision comes from new knowledge that generates new thoughts. So, vision is made by thoughts about how things or a situation should be. Vision makes the status quo obsolete, creates a sense of urgency, motivates change and activates people.

## First steps

The first steps start a process of change but there is a need for continuous and long-term actions to achieve the required sustainable change. Change is a long journey of many steps and it takes time to reach the destination. This is why **actions** and **time** are key factors in the equation of change. So, change requires actions and time.

## The resistance

Change and resistance are two sides of the same coin. There is always resistance to change. Like in Physics where motion creates friction, change naturally creates resistance. But there is a minimum force required to overcome friction. In the same way, to start change you need new knowledge and clear vision to overcome the resistance forces supporting the status quo. Despite resistance to change, change will happen when all the factors for change (**vision, people, action and time**) are valued, grown and combined.

Resistance to change is due to a lack of knowledge, information, or skills. It can also be due to negative attitudes and behaviours. Resistance can be addressed through education, training, communication and information or by addressing prejudices, assumptions, and perceptions.

# III. UNDESTANDING CHANGE

The word 'change' denotes a difference in anything observed over some period of time. Change is a natural law; it is a law of life. The only thing that does not change is change itself. Nothing is permanent and change is constant. Everything changes over time. Change is inevitable, we cannot stop it. Nothing stands still. By nature, human beings always desire change. Human beings are never satisfied with the conditions they live in; they are always looking for better living conditions. They want to change and succeed. The needs of human beings are changing day by day. So, to satisfy these needs they desire change. The only problem people have is to know the change they want and how to make it happen.

Changes can happen in different ways that affect human living conditions. Changes start in individual human beings at a personal level before being transferred to society in different domains, be it social, cultural, economic, political, technological or environmental. The main changes to be dealt with are: individual change or personal development, social change or transformation, human development, cultural change, economic development, political change, organisational or corporate change and technological change. These changes transform the society we live in every day.

## 3.1 Individual Change or Personal development

Changes start within individuals when they start to think differently and see things differently. People need to change to adapt to the changing environment that produces ever new challenges. Individuals cannot survive or dominate the new situation unless they equip themselves with new knowledge, skills and a strong will to overcome. Personal change can happen at the physical, mental, spiritual, emotional and professional level. People change their attitude and character. To influence others positively, people must first change themselves positively. Change requires new thinking. In order to change, people must learn the truth, get new knowledge, change their thoughts and start making different and better choices.

Individual change happens when a person grows and develops self-awareness, broadens their knowledge and competence base, improves their mental and spiritual health, and is able to examine assumptions, mindsets in order to make the right choices. Here is an example of the application of the Formula for Accelerated Change for a personal change:

**The Formula for Accelerated Change**

| Dr Myles Munroe[4]'s Vision | People | Actions | Time | Change |
|---|---|---|---|---|
| 'I exist to transform followers into leaders'. 'I want to die empty'. | One person: Dr Myles Munroe | Study, Read, Teach, Preach, Train, Mentor, Talk, write books, etc. | 1954-2014. | He changed himself and millions of people around the world. |

## 3.2 Human Development

Human development[5] is defined as the process of enlarging people's freedoms and opportunities and improving their well-being. Human development is about the real freedom ordinary people have to decide who to be, what to do, and how to live.

Development concerns expanding the choices people have, to lead lives that they value, and improving the human condition so that people have the chance to lead full lives. Thus, human development is about much more than economic growth, which is only a means of enlarging people's choices. Building human capabilities is fundamental to enlarging these choices – the range of things that people can do or be in life. Capabilities are 'the substantive freedoms a person enjoys to lead the kind of life they have reason to value.'

Human development disperses the concentration of the distribution of goods and services that underprivileged people need and centres its ideas on human decisions. By investing in people, we enable growth and empower people to pursue many different life paths, thus developing human capabilities. The most basic capabilities for human development are: to lead long and healthy lives, to be knowledgeable (e.g. to be educated), to have access to the resources and social services needed for a decent standard of living, and to be able to participate in the life of the community. Without these, many choices are simply not available, and many opportunities in life remain inaccessible.

There are six basic pillars of human development: equity, sustainability, productivity, empowerment, cooperation and security.

- Equity is the idea of fairness for every person; we each have the right to education and healthcare.

---

[4] Dr Myles Munroe (20 April 1954–9 November 2014) was a Bahamian Evangelical Christian evangelist, author of numerous books and inspirational and motivational speaker on leadership.
[5] Human Development definition provided on Wikipedia.

## The Formula for Accelerated Change

- Sustainability is the view that we all have the right to earn a living that can sustain our lives and have access to a more even distribution of goods.
- Productivity states the full participation of people in generating income. This also means that the government needs more efficient social programmes for its people.
- Empowerment is the freedom of people to influence development and decisions that affect their lives.
- Cooperation stipulates participation and belonging to communities and groups as a means of mutual enrichment and a source of social meaning.
- Security offers people development opportunities freely and safely with confidence that they will not disappear suddenly in the future.

Here is an example of a human development process guided by an organisational vision:

| Trócaire's[6] Vision | People | Actions | Time | Change |
|---|---|---|---|---|
| A just and peaceful world where people's dignity is ensured and rights are respected; where basic needs are met and resources are shared equitably; where people have control over their own lives and those in power act for the common good. | At least 300 people, Board, Committees, staff members of an international development organisation. | Sensitise, Mobilise, Teach, Train, Plan, Organise, Work, Talk, Campaign, Lobby, Fundraise, Support development projects and programmes, etc. | 42 years (1973-2015). | More than 50 million people living now in developing countries in Africa, Asia and Latin America have been changed. |

### 3.3 Social change or social transformation

Social change refers to the transformation of culture, behaviour, social institutions, and social structure over time. In the world we are aware that society is never static and that social, political, economic and cultural changes occur constantly. Social change happens when individuals and communities generate and tap into powerful new ideas.

One of the most powerful social changes in the world was produced by the Civil Rights Movement led by Martin Luther King Jr. in the United States of America. Even now people wonder how he did it. They wonder how an ordinary citizen without economic or political power led a successful movement against racism that deeply changed American society.

How Martin Luther King Jr. did it is demonstrated by the Formula for Accelerated Change. He shared a **vision** of equal rights for all American citizens, including African-Americans. **People** who

---

6 Trócaire is the Irish Catholic agency for International Development.

believed in what he believed in joined him and formed a movement which grew and reached the whole country. He and his followers carried out **actions** to bring more people on board and to influence other people to get involved. They pushed the government to change discriminatory laws to allow the desired change. It took **time** to make change happen; even now **changes** induced by his vision are still happening to fully achieve his vision. Despite lots of improvements, the United States of America is not yet free from racial inequalities. This is how the Formula for Accelerated Change applied with Martin Luther King's vision:

| Martin Luther King Jr.'s Vision | People | Actions | Time | Change |
|---|---|---|---|---|
| 'I have a dream that little black boys and black girls will join hands with white girls and boys and become sisters and brothers'. | At least 2,500 leaders joined the Civil rights movement in 1955. About 17,000 took part initially in the Montgomery Bus Boycott. | Study, Teach, Train, Preach, Plan, Organise, Work, Talk, Campaign, Lobby, March, Demonstrate, Boycott, Petition, write books and articles, etc. | 60 years (1955-2015). | More than 300 million people now living in the US and many outside have been changed. |

## 3.4 Cultural change

Cultural change is about transforming collective patterns of thinking and acting, changing the 'rules' and values that sustain patterns of exclusion, exploring and transforming collective habits of thinking, understanding and behaviour, and promoting a more inclusive, participatory culture of 'civic engagement'. The women's rights movement has produced one of the biggest cultural changes; this is how the Formula for Accelerated Change is applied to it:

| Vision | People | Actions | Time | Change |
|---|---|---|---|---|
| A world where there are equal rights and treatment of women and men. | Members of women's rights movement and associations. | Study, Teach, Train, Preach, Plan, Organise, Work, Talk, Mobilise, Campaign, Lobby, March, Demonstrate, Boycott, Support women, Change laws, etc. | From the 19th century until now. | Billions of women in the world have had their lives changed. |

## The Formula for Accelerated Change

### 3.5 Economic change

Economic change commonly known as economic development is the development of the economic wealth of countries, regions or communities for the well-being of their inhabitants. From a policy perspective, economic development can be defined as efforts that seek to improve the economic well-being and quality of life for a community by creating and/or retaining jobs and supporting or growing incomes and the tax base. Economic development is purely and simply the creation of wealth in which community benefits are created. Economic development improves the living standards of people. The Formula for Accelerated Change is applied to economic change as shown below:

| Vision | People | Actions | Time | Change |
|--------|--------|---------|------|--------|
| A country where everybody lives a decent life with a minimum income. | Local leaders from public, private and civil society. | Study, Teach, Train, Plan, Organise, Work, Talk, Mobilise, Campaign, Lobby, Adopt new policy and new laws, etc. | 10 to 20 years. | Millions of people have had their lives improved. |

### 3.6 Political change

Politics dictates how people are governed in countries. Governments establish political systems where laws, rules and regulations are set up to create spaces in which people exercise their rights to express and act in the search of happiness and prosperity. Unfortunately, some governments find it difficult to always come up with the best political systems that people expect. The democratic systems are established to allow people to give power to those who can rule and meet people's aspirations and expectations. In order to succeed governments have always to change their politics to respond to new environments, new challenges and the changing needs of the people.

Making effective political change that people need requires visionary leadership with a clear vision of where to guide people. The success of a political change will depend on how people embrace the formulated vision and move together in the same direction to achieve common goals.

In South Africa, Nelson Mandela expressed a vision to free South Africans from the racist regime of Apartheid. Analysed carefully, the political change produced in South Africa has followed the Formula for Accelerated Change as described here:

**The Formula for Accelerated Change**

| Nelson Mandela's Vision | People | Actions | Time | Change |
|---|---|---|---|---|
| 'I have cherished the ideal of a democratic and free society in which all persons will live together in harmony and with equal opportunities. It is an ideal for which I hope to live for and to see realised. But, My Lord, if it needs be, it is an ideal for which I am prepared to die.' Mandela, 1963. | About 100 ANC leaders in 1960. | Study, Teach, Train, Plan, Organise, Work, Talk, Campaign, Lobby, March, Demonstrate, Boycott, Civil disobedience, Petition, write books and articles, etc. | 55 years (1960-2015). | More than 50 million people living in South Africa and many outside have been changed. |

## 3.7 Organisational or corporate change

An organisation or corporate entity that does not change will die. Making the desired change for an organisation starts by creating a vision of what an organisation should be or where it should be heading. The translation of the vision into reality requires a visionary leadership that will share the vision with staff, board members and other stakeholders in the organisation; planning and implementing the actions necessary to move towards a fixed vision.

Organisational change happens when there are changes in structures, systems and procedures (constitutions, laws, policies, etc.). One of the most successful global companies is Coca-Cola. If we analyse its history, structures and achievement we see proof of the power of the vision and the support of the Formula for Accelerated Change as follows:

| Coca-Cola 's Vision | People | Actions | Time | Change |
|---|---|---|---|---|
| 'The undisputed leader in every market in which we compete'. | Board members, bottlers, distributors and employees (130,600 in 2013). | Study, Train, Plan, Organise, Work, Produce, Market, Publicise, etc. | 129 years (1886-2015). | About 1.7 billion people consume Coca-Cola products around the world every day. |

## 3.8 Technological change

New technologies are affecting all aspects of lives in the world. Technology is the application of scientific knowledge to the making of tools to solve specific problems. Technological advances such as automobiles, airplanes, radio, television, cellular phones, computers, modems, and fax machines have brought major advances and changes to the world. Indeed, since the last century technology

## The Formula for Accelerated Change

has completely – and irreversibly – changed the way people meet, interact, learn, work, play, travel, worship, and do business.

Technological changes have impacted different areas of human life and produced changes at personal, economic, social, and environmental levels. But to produce the desired change in other areas, the application of technologies has to be carefully done to avoid the negative outcomes that some technologies could bring.

The computer and internet are the inventions that have made huge technological changes. One of the greatest technological leaders is Bill Gates, who developed the computer software that is used in most personal computers. His vision was simple but proved to be powerful 'A computer on each desk and in each home'. He said that when a computer of less than one gigabyte (GB) was as big as a five-storey building. Here is how the Formula for Accelerated Change is applied to the change made by Microsoft.

| Bill Gates[7] Vision | People | Actions | Time | Change |
|---|---|---|---|---|
| 'A computer on each desk and in each home' | About 10 people were involved in Microsoft when Bill Gates got the first contract. | Study, Learn, Plan, Organise, Negotiate, Teach, Train, Work Develop software, Market, Sell, etc. | 35 years (1980-2015). | Now more than one billion people use the internet and Microsoft software on their personal computers. |

### What the great leaders say about Change:

'You must be the change you wish to see in the world.' Mahatma Gandhi

'Progress is impossible without change, and those who cannot change their minds cannot change anything.' George Bernard Shaw

'We never change things by fighting the existing reality. To change something, build a new model that makes the existing model obsolete.' Richard Buckminster Fuller

'Change is the law of life. And those who look only to the past or present are certain to miss the future.' John F. Kennedy

'Change favours the prepared mind.' Louis Pasteur

'If you do not change direction, you may end up where you are heading.' Lao Tzu

---

[7] Bill Gates, is the founder of Microsoft.

Juvenal TURATINZE

## The Formula for Accelerated Change

'To improve is to change; to be perfect is to change often.' Winston Churchill

'Change does not roll in on the wheels of inevitability, but comes through continuous struggle. And so we must straighten our backs and work for our freedom. A man can't ride you unless your back is bent.' Martin Luther King, Jr.

'When we are no longer able to change a situation - we are challenged to change ourselves.' Viktor E. Frankl

'There is nothing permanent except change.' Heraclitus

'People don't resist change. They resist being changed!' Peter Senge

'Everyone thinks of changing the world, but no one thinks of changing himself.' Leo Tolstoy

'Education is the most powerful weapon you can use to change the world.' Nelson Mandela

'Some men see things as they are and say, 'Why?' I dream of things that never were and say, 'Why not?' George Bernard Shaw

'Never doubt that a small, group of thoughtful, committed citizens can change the world.' Margaret Mead

'If you don't like the way the world is, you change it. You have an obligation to change it. You just do it one step at a time.' Marian Wright Edelman

'People generally fall into one of three groups: the few who make things happen, the many who watch things happen, and the overwhelming majority who have no notion of what happens. Every person is either a creator of fact or a creature of circumstance. He either puts colour into his environment, or, like a chameleon, takes colour from his environment.' Dr Myles Munroe

# IV. HOW THE FORMULA FOR ACCELERATED CHANGE WORKS

Change happens every time at personal level, change happens in a family, in a group, in a community, in an organisation, in a company, in a nation and in the world. The key question we often have is how we make the positive change in our lives. Below are examples on how changes are made by applying the Formula for Accelerated Change at different levels.

## 4.1 Types of changes

### Personal change

As a person, changing yourself starts by creating a vision of who you should be or you want to be. A vision which is rooted in what you believe. When you are committed to your vision, you believe in challenging the status quo and start to think differently. When you start thinking differently, your behaviours change and you start to initiate the new actions required to take you to your vision. With a strong vision and strong beliefs in yourself, you never quit and with time you will succeed in achieving your vision and make a new life.

| Vision | People | Actions | Time | Change |
|--------|--------|---------|------|--------|
| I am a successful person who meets all my needs and helps other people. | One person. | Plan, Study, Work, Exercise Learn, Love, Laugh, etc. | Five years. | My living standard is improved and all my needs are satisfied. |

### Change in a family

A family is made up of a husband, a wife and children. Parents are responsible for building a successful family that will leave a good legacy to their children. Family changes all the time right from the first day of marriage, but to get the desired change a family needs to have a vision. This vision has to come from the husband or the wife, but has to be shared by both in order to have a family that will function effectively towards it. Once both parents have a common vision of the family they want to build, they will have to instil this vision in their children and teach them how to think, behave and act to achieve the desired vision. With the vision in mind, appropriate actions become routines or rituals done regularly to build a better future and legacy.

### The Formula for Accelerated Change

The Formula for Accelerated Change proves that two people with a common vision can influence at least other two people to achieve change in four people. So, when a husband and a wife have a common good vision for their family, they will automatically influence their children positively. When their child reaches a stage of getting and owning the vision, they will all influence each other. In short, a successful family needs a common vision, a plan of action to implement over a period of time to achieve the desired change.

| Vision | People | Actions | Time | Change |
|---|---|---|---|---|
| A successful and loving family where everybody is happy and fulfils his potential and inspires others. | Two to Ten persons: a Husband father, a wife/mother and children. | Plan, Teach, Train Study, Read, work, help each other, Exercise, Learn, Love, Laugh, etc. | 25 years. | All family members have a fulfilled life and many more people (4 to 100) will be influenced and have a new life. |

### Making change in a group or a team

A group or a team is an assembly of people with a common purpose. Members of the group should know why their group exists or the purpose of coming together. To effectively achieve the desired results any group has to start by fixing a common vision and doing collective actions. This vision could come from an individual but has to be shared among members to become the group's vision.

The Formula for Accelerated Change shows that a number of people with a common vision will inevitably influence the number of followers times squared. For example 10 members of a group who share a common vision and do collective actions to achieve that vision will attract and influence at least another 100 people.

| Vision | People | Actions | Time | Change |
|---|---|---|---|---|
| We are all healthy physically and spiritually. | Ten people. | Plan, Teach, Train, Study, Exercise, Read, Learn, Love, Laugh, Work, Help each other and help other people, etc. | One year. | At least 100 persons have a healthy life physically and spiritually. |

### Making change in a community

A community is a social group of any size whose members reside in a specific locality, share government, and often have a common cultural and historical heritage. Change always happens in

# The Formula for Accelerated Change

any community. But to achieve a desired change in a community, members must have a common vision that could come from one member but is shared with other members.

According to the Formula for Accelerated Change, if two people share a vision they can influence four; three can influence nine, etc. Always the number of people with a common vision will inevitably influence at least the number of followers times squared. So, making change in a community requires a vision, a critical mass of people who share the vision, a plan of actions to be implemented over time to get the expected results or impact.

| Vision | People | Actions | Time | Change |
|--------|--------|---------|------|--------|
| We are free from poverty and our human rights are respected. | 100 people | Plan, Learn, Train, Create employment, Do businesses, Work, Campaign, Help each other and help other people, etc. | 10 years. | At least 10,000 persons have a decent life physically, economically, socially, etc. |

## Making change in an organisation or a company

Organisations or companies are created for a purpose that defines why they exist. The reason behind the purpose is to make change in the society they operate in. Some organisations or companies succeed and others fail. The causes of failures could be many but the unique and ultimate cause of failure of an organisation or company is the lack of a shared vision among its members or staff.

Many organisations or companies wrongly emphasise what they do and how they do it. They have mission statements that are inward looking, that define what they want to do and what they want to become, and forget that the most important thing is why they exist. The key is the vision they believe in, everything else follows.

According to the Formula for Accelerated Change, in order for an organisation or a company to succeed and make the desired change it needs to have an organisation vision, a critical mass of people at all levels, a collective plan of actions to be implemented over time.

| Vision | People | Actions | Time | Change |
|--------|--------|---------|------|--------|
| Everyone living in our city to have decent housing. | 500 people. | Plan, Work, Increase income, save money, Talk to authorities, negotiate with banks, Get loans, Campaign, Teach, Train, Produce building materials, Help each other and help other people, etc. | 10 years. | At least 250,000 people's lives improved with decent housing. |

Juvenal TURATINZE

## The Formula for Accelerated Change

### Making change in a nation

A nation is a large body of people united by common descent, history, culture, or language, inhabiting a particular country or territory. People in a nation are interdependent and share the same destiny. Nations create states to govern their people. Established governments work to improve the well-being of the people. Clearly the purpose of governments is to lead people to changes that improve their lives.

History shows that many nations have failed to achieve permanent positive changes in the lives of people and millions of people still live in absolute poverty.

The destructions or failures of nations are mainly due to the lack of a common vision. When people who live together lack a common vision and purpose, their actions collide and destroy each other. But in a nation where people share the same vision, the same beliefs and dreams, it becomes easier to initiate actions individually or collectively towards the common good.

According to the Formula for Accelerated Change, a nation or a country succeeds if its leadership creates a national vision, mobilises at least a critical (mass) number of its citizens who embrace that vision and collectively commit to implement action plans over a period of time to get the expected results.

For example, in a country of 12 million people, you need at least 3,465 people committed to achieving the national vision and to implement collective plans of actions over a fixed period of time. Many national governments around the world elaborate national visions to guide their development. Rwanda is a good example of how a national vision can steer transformation. A national vision, known as Vision 2020, was created in 2000 and through national debates and people's mobilisation it was shared among citizens at all levels. Since 2000, Vision 2020 has guided the design of Economic Development and Poverty Reduction Strategies (EDPRS) and actions plans in all sectors and at all levels. The outcomes realised so far ensure that the targeted indicators will be reached by 2020. This is a good example of how the Formula for Accelerated Change works in making change that brings national transformation.

## The Formula for Accelerated Change

| Rwanda's Vision 2020 | People | Actions | Time | Change |
|---|---|---|---|---|
| 'To transform our country into a middle-income nation in which Rwandans are healthier, educated and generally more prosperous. | Rwandans in leadership (minimum 3,500 people). | Study, Teach, Train, Plan, Work, Produce, Build infrastructure, Create businesses, Increase income, Make savings, Invest, Provide social services, Help each other, etc. | 20 years. | A poverty rate of less than 30 % in 2020 from a rate of 60.4 % in 2000. At least 4 million people lifted above the poverty line. |

### Making change in the world

Most people dream of changing the world. This is not impossible because history tells us about people who changed the world with their vision and actions. The people we know who made great impact in the world had one thing in common; they created a big vision that they shared with other people in different parts of the world. With their visions and beliefs, they did things that inspired many people who believed in what they believed and decided to follow them and to act alike. Among other people known to have influenced and changed the world, there are Mahatma Gandhi, Martin Luther King, Nelson Mandela, Steve Jobs, etc.

According to the Formula for Accelerated Change, changing the world requires a strong vision that digs deep into people's beliefs, a critical mass of people and actions all over the world to be implemented over time. The critical mass of people you need now is not as big as we may think. We need less than 83,667 people with a common vision to influence 7 billion people. This is not impossible. We have good examples like the growth of the Christian religion. Jesus Christ first shared his vision of the church with only 12 people and 2,000 years later there are 2.2 billion Christians worldwide. Christianity is a good example that explains and proves the Formula for Accelerated Change at international level.

The vision of human dignity of Mahatma Gandhi changed the lives of millions of Indians. The vision of civil rights activists, with their leader, Martin Luther King Jr., changed millions of lives in the United States of America. Recently, the visions for the use of computers and information technologies, introduced by people like Bill Gates and Steve Jobs, have changed the lives of billions of people throughout the world.

**The Formula for Accelerated Change**

| Vision | People | Actions | Time | Change |
|---|---|---|---|---|
| A world free from hunger and poverty. | 50,000 people. | Study, Teach, Train, Plan, Work, Produce, Create jobs, Increase income, Make savings, Invest, Lobby , Advocate, Donate, Campaign, support, etc. | 15 years (2015-2030). | More than 2.5 billion have access to food and meet other basic needs. |

## 4.2 Measuring and calculating change using the formula

In order to measure and calculate change with the formula $(V \times P^2 \times A \times T = C)$, we need to find ways of assigning figures to the factors of the formula: vision, people, actions, and time.

### Measuring change

The **change** desired consists of improved lives or new lives produced through a process of change. The number of new lives determines the importance and the level of impact of change. The result of change is measured by the number of new lives produced. The new lives are the improved lives of people in a specific area of life in which the change happens to fulfil the defined vision.

### Measuring vision

**Vision** is not easy to measure. However, in this formula the magnitude of vision is estimated and given a value. We define three levels of vision, namely a small vision (V1), average vision (V2) and a big and global vision (V3) with a value of 1, 2 and 3 respectively.

| Vision | Value | Type of Vision |
|---|---|---|
| V1 : Small vision | 1 | Vision for an individual, a family, a group or an association, that targets less than 1,000 people. |
| V2: Average Vision | 2 | Vision: vision for a community, an institution, a corporate or a country, that targets between 1,000 and 100 million people. |
| V3: Big and global Vision | 3 | Vision for the world that targets more than 100 million people. |

### Measuring people

**People** are those individuals that have embraced the vision and are taking actions to achieve it. They are engaged and have a plan of actions to implement over a fixed time. The greater the number of people in an action, the more the change will happen. More visionary people will influence more people. Having a common vision produces a synergy that creates an exponential effect on the capacity of people to influence each other and achieve. That is why the 'people'" factor is squared.

# The Formula for Accelerated Change

For personal change, there is one individual in an action, but for a group, an organisation, a corporate entity, a country or the world there are many individuals in an action.

## Measuring actions

**Actions** are measured by being given a value depending on their levels. There are first step actions (A1), second step actions (A2) and third step actions (A3), with a value of 1, 2 and 3 respectively.

| Actions | Value | Type of actions |
|---|---|---|
| A1 : First step actions | 1 | First strategic plan of actions |
| A2 : Second step actions | 2 | Second strategic plan of actions |
| A3: Third step actions | 3 | Third strategic plan of actions |

## Measuring Time

In the formula, time is measured in generations. There is first generation (T1), second generation (T2) and third generation (T3).

| Time | Value | Period |
|---|---|---|
| T1 : First time generation | 1 | 0 to 50 years |
| T2 : Second time generation | 2 | 50 to 100 years |
| T3: Third time generation | 3 | From 100 years and beyond |

## Calculating personal change

| Vision | People | Actions | Time | Change |
|---|---|---|---|---|
| Vision | One individual | First step actions | First generation | New life |
| 1 | 1 | 1 | 1 | 1 |
| A visionary individual takes actions and changes his/her own life over a period of less than 20 years. | | | | |

## Calculating change in a family, a group or an association

| Vision | People | Actions | Time | Change |
|---|---|---|---|---|
| Vision | 10 individuals | First step actions | First generation | New lives |
| 1 | 10 | 1 | 1 | 100 |
| 10 individuals in a family, a group or an association with a common vision will carry out actions that will improve lives their member individuals in less than 20 years. | | | | |

Juvenal TURATINZE

**The Formula for Accelerated Change**

## Calculating change in a community or a corporate entity

| Vision | People | Actions | Time | Change |
|--------|--------|---------|------|--------|
| Vision | 50 individuals | Second step actions | First generation | New lives |
| 2 | 50 | 2 | 1 | 10,000 |
| Fifty individuals in a community, an institution or a corporate entity with a common vision will carry out actions that will improve the lives of at least 10,000 individuals in less than 20 years. | | | | |

## Calculating change in a country

| Vision | People | Actions | Time | Change |
|--------|--------|---------|------|--------|
| Vision | 2,000 individuals | Second step actions | First generation | New lives |
| 2 | 2,000 | 2 | 1 | 16,000,000 |
| 2,000 individuals in a country with a common vision will carry out actions (second step) that will improve the lives of at least 16,000,000 individuals in less than 20 years. | | | | |

## Calculating change in the world

| Vision | People | Actions | Time | Change |
|--------|--------|---------|------|--------|
| Vision | 10,000 individuals | Third step actions | Second generation | New lives |
| 3 | 10,000 | 3 | 2 | 1,800,000,000 |
| 10,000 individuals in the world with a common vision will carry out actions (third step) that will improve the lives of at least 1,800,000,000 individuals in less than 100 years (second generation). | | | | |

## 4.3 The right environment of change

Like a seed, things can only grow or develop in the right environment. In the same way change needs the right environment to happen. There should be a favourable environment that creates good conditions to allow development or growth to happen. A seed needs good soil with the right moisture, temperature, light and time to germinate and grow. The right combination of all these elements is necessary for the seeds to grow, become a tree and ultimately bear fruit.

For change to happen the right environment is needed for its elements or ingredients (vision, people and actions) to grow. These elements all combined require the right environment to develop and produce change. However, the right environment is not always there, that is why people should strive to create a fostering and sustainable environment where change can happen and prosper. Leaders are responsible for creating the right environment for the desired change to happen.

## The Formula for Accelerated Change

Like a farmer who prepares and works the soil for his seeds, who ensures that there is enough moisture and that the temperature is right and that there is adequate sunlight for the seed to become a tree and bear fruits, so too a leader prepares the people who will take on his vision, plans and carries out actions to produce change over time.

# V. DEVELOPING AND MIXING THE INGREDIENTS OF CHANGE

Making change is like making bread you need ingredients. In bread-making, you need wheat flour, water, sugar, salt and yeast. First, wheat has to be grown and processed to make flour, yeast has to be grown, water has to be treated and purified, sugar cane or sugar beet have to be grown and processed to make sugar, and salt has to be collected from the sea and treated; then these ingredients are gathered and mixed to make dough. The dough is given time for the yeast to work before being put in the oven or on the fire to be cooked and become bread.

Like bread-making, change-making needs ingredients, namely: vision, people, actions and time. These ingredients have to be grown and processed as well and gotten ready to be used.

There are elements necessary for each ingredient (factor) to grow and get ready to be used and produce change. These elements are presented in the table below:

| Vision | People | Actions | Time |
|---|---|---|---|
| Purpose<br>Thoughts<br>Ideas<br>Knowledge<br>Imagination<br>Positive thinking<br>Creativity<br>Innovation<br>New mindset<br>Paradigm shift | Self-awareness<br>Conscience<br>Character<br>Attitude<br>Beliefs and values<br>Self-discipline<br>Dignity<br>Leadership<br>Empowerment<br>Mentoring<br>Team building<br>Empathy<br>Dialogue<br>Synergy<br>Critical mass | Independent will<br>Responsibility<br>Initiative<br>Action planning<br>Proactivity<br>Prioritising<br>Organising<br>Speaking<br>Entrepreneurship | Time Management<br>Past<br>Present<br>Future |
| **Change**<br>Personal, Organisational, Social, Cultural, Political, Economic, Technological, etc. | | | |

Ingredients are mixed with their respective elements or combined to work on each other over time to produce the desired change as a final product.

Juvenal TURATINZE

**The Formula for Accelerated Change**

### 5.1 Vision

Vision is very powerful. The bible says: 'where there is no vision people perish'. Without a vision, the whole of society is doomed to a catastrophic end. An individual without a vision is predestined for failure or a meaningless and worthless life. A vision gives focus to life.

A vision is an image of how things should be. This image is made by a mental imagination guided by the heart. Vision is different from sight. Sight is the function of the eye, but vision is the function of the heart and the mind together. Vision requires passion from the heart, a conviction and a strong desire to fulfil one's own or people's potential.

The mind translates the desire into a dream and a future reality. Having a vision is about making choices of what you want to become in the future. Leaders believe in their vision and equip themselves to achieve it.

In order to advance it is very important for an individual to have a personal vision, for a community to have a collective vision and for a country to have a national vision. To translate vision into reality there is a need for leadership that generates a strong will to change things.

When a person or a group is led by a person without a vision, the result is disorder, confusion and anarchy. Therefore, you should have a clear vision of where to go and be dedicated with all your heart to achieving your vision.

When we speak of a clear mental picture, we may as well say that it is a picture that we keep playing in our mind about the outcome of the future.

A vision includes visual reality, an internal still portrait, which at this moment doesn't exist. It is not somebody else's view of the future but is exclusively your personal experiential view.

Consequently, if you want to materialise this picture for others, you should draw or paint it for others to see. The same is true when you use your imagination to create a dream. You will be able to lead others to seize your vision so that you can share it with them. Therefore, it is very important to have a clear picture. An unclear perspective is not a vision.

What is important to know about vision is that it always brings about change. It never keeps the status quo. The vision focuses on the future and doesn't try to reproduce the past.

The vision actually stretches the reality beyond the present status. Without a clear vision to keep people on target, you could end up with problem people who are fighting and who resist change.

### The Formula for Accelerated Change

Leadership requires vision. Leadership is having a vision and being able to articulate it so that people around you can understand it and arrive at a consensus on a common vision. It is a force that provides meaning and purpose to the work. Leaders of change are visionary leaders, and vision is the basis of their work. They begin with a personal vision to forge a shared vision with other people. A vision ignites people. The communication of a vision is such that it empowers people to act. A visionary leadership is dynamic and involves a three-stage process: (i) an image of the desired future (vision) is (ii) communicated (shared) which serves to (iii) 'empower' followers so that they can enact the vision.

A vision needs to be created and developed in order to direct the course of change. In conjunction with the vision, a strategic action should be designed to achieve the vision. An effective vision should be imaginable, desirable, feasible, focused, flexible and communicable.

### What the great leaders say about Vision:

'Where there is no vision the people perish.' Bible (Proverbs 29:18)

'Purpose is when you know and understand what you were born to accomplish. Vision is when you see it in your mind and begin to imagine it.' Dr Myles Munroe

'Vision without execution is hallucination.' Thomas Edison

'Vision without action is only dreaming, action without vision is only passing time, vision with action can change the world.' Nelson Mandela

'Dream lofty dreams, and as you dream, so shall you become. Your Vision is the promise of what you shall one day be. Your ideal is the prophecy of what you shall at last unveil.'
James Allen

'Dissatisfaction and discouragement are not caused by the absence of things but the absence of vision.' Anonymous

'The most pathetic person in the world is someone who has sight, but has no vision.'
Helen Keller

'The man doesn't make the vision; the vision makes the man.' Pastor Yonggi Cho

'Vision is the art of seeing the invisible.' Jonathan Swift

## The Formula for Accelerated Change

> 'A vision is not just a picture of what could be; it is an appeal to our better selves, a call to become something more.' Rosabeth Moss Kanter
>
> 'To grasp and hold a vision, that is the very essence of successful leadership—not only on the movie set where I learned it, but everywhere.' Ronald Reagan
>
> 'Leadership is the capacity to translate vision into reality.' Warren Bennis
>
> 'I think that the greatest gift God ever gave man is not the gift of sight but the gift of vision.' Dr Myles Munroe
>
> ' 'Purpose is when you know and understand what you were born to accomplish. Vision is when you see it in your mind and begin to imagine it.' Dr Myles Munroe

### 5.1.1 Purpose

A personal vision gives a life purpose. For an individual or an organisation, the purpose is the fundamental reason for being. Purpose should not be confused with goals and objectives. Whereas you might achieve a goal or an objective, you cannot fulfil a purpose or a vision; it is like a guiding star on the horizon forever pursued, but never reached. Yet while purpose itself does not change, it does inspire change. The very fact that purpose can never be fully realised means that an individual or an organisation can never stop stimulating change and progress in order to live up more fully to its purpose.

We must know how to live life with purpose in order to make the change we desire.

Here are elements that bind a life with purpose:

- **Live by your beliefs and values.** People who live a life of purpose have core beliefs and values that influence their decisions, shape their day-to-day actions, and determine their short- and long-term priorities.
- **Set priorities.** People who live a life of purpose identify those activities that matter most to them and spend the majority of their time and effort in those areas.
- **Follow your passion.** People who live a life of purpose wake up each morning eager to face the new day. They pursue their dreams, put their heart into everything they do, and feel that they're personally making a difference.
- **Achieve balance.** People who live a life of purpose put their heart into their career and to building relationships with friends and family. They also reserve adequate time to satisfy

**The Formula for Accelerated Change**

their personal needs. Achieving balance means living up to one's potential in all facets of life.

- **Feel content.** People who live a life of purpose have an inner peace. They're satisfied with what they have and who they are.
- **Make a difference.** People who live a life of purpose make a meaningful difference in someone else's life. They do things for others without any expectation of personal gain, serve as exemplary role models, and gain as much satisfaction from witnessing the success of others as witnessing their own.
- **Live in the moment.** People who live a life of purpose cherish every moment and seek to live life without regret. They take joy in the experiences that life gives and don't worry about keeping score.

**What the great leaders say about Purpose:**

'The main purpose of life is to live rightly, think rightly, act rightly. The soul must languish when we give all our thought to the body.' Mahatma Gandhi

'There is one quality which one must possess to win, and that is definiteness of purpose, the knowledge of what one wants, and a burning desire to possess it.' Napoleon Hill

'Our prime purpose in this life is to help others. And if you can't help them, at least don't hurt them.' Dalai Lama

'Law and order exist for the purpose of establishing justice and when they fail in this purpose they become the dangerously structured dams that block the flow of social progress.' Martin Luther King, Jr.

'The purpose of life is to live it, to taste experience to the utmost, to reach out eagerly and without fear for newer and richer experience.' Eleanor Roosevelt

'Work gives you meaning and purpose and life is empty without it.' Stephen Hawking

'The purpose of life is to live, learn, and love.' Christine Rice

'People who use time wisely spend it on activities that advance their overall purpose in life.' John C. Maxwell

'The purpose of a business is to create a customer.' Peter Drucker

**The Formula for Accelerated Change**

### 5.1.2 Thoughts

A thought is an idea or opinion produced by thinking, or that occurs suddenly in the mind. Your thoughts become your beliefs which result in your actions. Your actions are the practical manifestations of your thoughts. The nature of your thoughts determines the quality of your life. Changing your thoughts can change your life. Change happens with new thoughts.

**What the great leaders say about Thoughts:**

> 'A man is but the product of his thoughts what he thinks, he becomes.' Mahatma Gandhi
>
> 'Change your thoughts and you change the world.' Norman Vincent Peale
>
> 'Whether you think you can or think you can't, you are right.' Henry Ford
>
> 'The significant problems we face cannot be solved at the same level of thinking we were at when we created them.' Albert Einstein
>
> 'Life is one big road with lots of signs. So when you are riding through the ruts, don't complicate your mind. Flee from hate, mischief and jealousy. Don't bury your thoughts; put your vision to reality. Wake Up and Live!' Bob Marley
>
> 'Great thoughts speak only to the thoughtful mind, but great actions speak to all mankind.' Theodore Roosevelt
>
> "Once you replace negative thoughts with positive ones, you'll start having positive results." Willie Nelson

### 5.1.3 New ideas

An idea is a thought or a collection of thoughts that generate in the mind. An idea is usually generated with intent, but can also be created unintentionally. Ideas often form during brainstorming sessions or through discussions. To generate new ideas, people need to open their mind and think differently.

All of us can tend to get stuck in certain thinking patterns. Breaking these thought patterns can help you get your mind unstuck and generate new ideas. There are several techniques you can use to break established thought patterns:

- **Challenge assumptions:** For every situation, you have a set of key assumptions. Challenging these assumptions gives you a whole new spin on possibilities.

Juvenal TURATINZE

**The Formula for Accelerated Change**

- **Reword the problem:** Stating the problem differently often leads to different ideas. To reword the problem look at the issue from different angles. 'Why do we need to solve the problem?', 'What's the roadblock here?', 'What will happen if we don't solve the problem?' These questions will give you new insights. You might come up with new ideas to solve your new problem.

- **Think in reverse:** If you feel you cannot think of anything new, try turning things upside-down. Instead of focusing on how you could solve a problem/improve operations/enhance a product, consider how you could create the problem/worsen operations/downgrade the product. The opposite ideas will come flowing in. Consider these ideas – once you've reversed them again – as possible solutions for the original challenge.

- **Express yourself through different media:** We have multiple intelligences but somehow, when faced with workplace challenges we just tend to use our verbal reasoning ability. How about expressing the challenge through different media – clay, music, word association games, paint? There are several ways you can express the challenge. Don't bother about solving the challenge at this point. Just express it. Different expressions might spark off different thought patterns. And these new thought patterns may yield new ideas.

**What the great leaders say about Ideas:**

'There is nothing as powerful as an idea. Everything created began as an idea. Ideas created and control the world. Pursue divine ideas.' Dr Myles Munroe

'For an idea that does not seem insane, there is no hope.' Albert Einstein

'I can't understand why people are frightened of new ideas. I'm frightened of old ones.' John Cage

'The best way to have a good idea is to have a lot of ideas.' Linus Pauling

'An idea that is not dangerous is unworthy of being called an idea at all.' Oscar Wilde

'Creative thinking inspires ideas. Ideas inspire change.' Barbara Januszkiewicz

'Great minds discuss ideas; average minds discuss events; small minds discuss people.' Eleanor Roosevelt

'If I have a thousand ideas and only one turns out to be good, I am satisfied.' Alfred Nobel

## The Formula for Accelerated Change

'Ideas shape the course of history.' John Maynard Keynes

'The role of a creative leader is not to have all the ideas; it's to create a culture where everyone can have ideas and feel that they're valued.' Ken Robinson

'Software innovation, like almost every other kind of innovation, requires the ability to collaborate and share ideas with other people, and to sit down and talk with customers and get their feedback and understand their needs.' Bill Gates

'The ideas I stand for are not mine. I borrowed them from Socrates. I swiped them from Chesterfield. I stole them from Jesus. And I put them in a book. If you don't like their rules, whose would you use?' Dale Carnegie

'To turn really interesting ideas and fledgling technologies into a company that can continue to innovate for years, it requires a lot of disciplines.' Steve Jobs

'Just as our eyes need light in order to see, our minds need ideas in order to conceive.' Napoleon Hill

'This is important: to get to know people, listen, expand the circle of ideas. The world is crisscrossed by roads that come closer together and move apart, but the important thing is that they lead towards the Good.' Pope Francis

'It is always better to have no ideas than false ones; to believe nothing, than to believe what is wrong.' Thomas Jefferson

'One can resist the invasion of an army but one cannot resist the invasion of ideas. Victor Hugo

'Ideas are the beginning points of all fortunes.' Napoleon Hill

'Ideas have a short shelf life. You must act on them before the expiration date.' John C. Maxwell

### 5.1.4 New knowledge

Knowledge is a familiarity, awareness or understanding of someone or something, such as facts, information, descriptions, or skills, which is acquired through experience or education by perceiving, discovering, or learning. Knowledge can refer to a theoretical or practical understanding of a subject.

**The Formula for Accelerated Change**

Knowledge acquisition involves complex cognitive processes: perception, communication, and reasoning. Knowledge is also said to be related to the capacity of acknowledgment in human beings.

When we think about knowledge the first thing that comes to mind is education. We believe that knowledge comes to people by their experiences in life. In other words, life is an instrument that leads us to gain knowledge. Many people consider that old people are wise because they have learned from good and bad experiences throughout their lives. Education requires work, dedication and faith to gain knowledge. We acquire knowledge through the guidance of parents, role models, college/university teachers and life experiences, etc.

### What the great leaders say about Knowledge:

'Knowledge is power. Information is liberating. Education is the premise of progress, in every society, in every family.' Kofi Annan

'A good decision is based on knowledge and not on numbers.' Plato

'To know is to know that you know nothing. That is the meaning of true knowledge.' Socrates

'To know what you know and what you do not know, that is true knowledge.' Confucius

'Today knowledge has power. It controls access to opportunity and advancement.' Peter Drucker

'Information is not knowledge.' Albert Einstein

'Without knowledge action is useless and knowledge without action is futile.' Abu Bakr

'Beware of false knowledge; it is more dangerous than ignorance.' George Bernard Shaw

'An investment in knowledge pays the best interest.' Benjamin Franklin

'The only source of knowledge is experience.' Albert Einstein

'The goal of education is the advancement of knowledge and the dissemination of truth.' John F. Kennedy

'There is one quality which one must possess to win, and that is definiteness of purpose, the knowledge of what one wants, and a burning desire to possess it.' Napoleon Hill

> 'I had rather excel others in the knowledge of what is excellent, than in the extent of my power and dominion.' Alexander the Great
>
> 'An empowered organisation is one in which individuals have the knowledge, skill, desire, and opportunity to personally succeed in a way that leads to collective organisational success.'
> Stephen Covey

## 5.1.5 Imagination

Imagination is the faculty or action of forming new ideas, or images or concepts not present in the senses or never before wholly perceived in reality.

Imagination is an integral part of the human mind that covers both the creative and learning spheres. Increasing one's imagination creates possibilities. It is considered to be the creative faculty of the mind that helps a person to process focused activities, such as thinking, memorising, remembering, or opinion forming. A rich imagination can enable you to pursue and accomplish many great things. There are various ways to enrich your imagination.

All human beings have been given the potential to develop a powerful 'creative imagination' to use for our own benefit and possibly the benefit of all mankind. Everything mankind has achieved throughout its existence is a result of its 'human imagination'.

Throughout the history of mankind, creative people have used their imagination to invent new verbal languages, innovations, art, stories, customs, religions, writing, and new technologies to solve problems.

Here are ten ways to increase imagination for better creative thinking:

• **Open your mind to unexplored paths.** Creativity is often tagged together with originality. To come up with new ideas may be challenging and even often daunting, as unexplored paths may pose unexpected threats. It is also an avenue where one can find genuine ideas that can result in a successful endeavour.

• **Read more.** Creativity and imagination are sparked by learning. One's willingness to learn new things gauges one's ability to accept and adapt to change. It improves one's adaptability to imaginative reasoning and creative thinking.

**The Formula for Accelerated Change**

• **Tell stories.** People love to listen to stories and each person has a story to tell. Practice imaginative and creative thinking by telling as many stories as you can. Let your story telling be descriptive. Let it allow you and your listener to visualise what is being told. Visualisation is an important part of increasing imagination. Visualisation is often perceived as one's ability to create a clear and vivid picture in the mind. Yet this concept entails various senses as well. Visualisation also involves one's sense of touch, smell, taste, and other senses. Visualisation enables you to imagine the story being told or the object being described. The more imaginative and creative the mind becomes, the more elaborate one's visualisations can be.

• **Be curious.** Learning new things sparks creativity and increases imagination. Part of learning new things is being curious. Children tend to be more imaginative because of their curious nature. Our inherent nature to seek answers or to learn new things does not disappear with age. Feed curiosity by learning and experiencing new things and notice how your imagination improves. Feed your curiosity by asking questions and build your ideas with the help of insight from others.

• **Don't be afraid to try something new.** It is often said that if you keep on doing the same things, then you will keep on receiving the same things. Challenge yourself to experience new things or embark on new adventures and endeavours.

• **Expand your interests.** Creativity is fuelled by passion. Expand your interests by shifting your focus to include other interests that you may be passionate about.

• **Develop your talents.** Everyone has a set of skills or talents. Focus on developing and honing these talents to express your creativity and imagination in areas that you excel in or in things that you know how to do best.

• **Spend time with creative people.** Synergise your energies by spending time with people who share the same interests as you. Brainstorming, planning, or simply talking to people will keep the creative juices running, giving new and fresh ideas.

• **Look at things differently.** When you feel tired or bored, and, and you feel that your creativity is running low, look at things from a new perspective. This will give you a fresh approach to things that may even trigger new ideas that you once thought to be impossible.

• **Condition your mind to relax through meditation techniques.** A well-rested mind has a higher potential to learn new things and come up with more creative ideas. There are various meditation methods that you can adopt to help increase imagination.

**The Formula for Accelerated Change**

**What the great leaders say about Imagination:**

'The true sign of intelligence is not knowledge but imagination.' Albert Einstein

'Imagination is the beginning of creation.' George Bernard Shaw

'Imagination rules the world.' Napoleon Bonaparte

'Everything you can imagine is real.' Pablo Picasso

'All successful people men and women are big dreamers. They imagine what their future could be, ideal in every respect, and then they work every day toward their distant vision, that goal or purpose.' Brian Tracy

'First comes thought; then organization of that thought, into ideas and plans; then transformation of those plans into reality. The beginning, as you will observe, is in your imagination.' Napoleon Hill

'Disneyland will never be completed. It will continue to grow as long as there is imagination left in the world.' Walt Disney

'Logic will get you from A to B. Imagination will take you everywhere.' Albert Einstein

'The level of our success is limited only by our imagination and no act of kindness, however small, is ever wasted.' Aesop

'Every human has four endowments – self-awareness, conscience, independent will and creative imagination. These give us the ultimate human freedom. The power to choose, to respond, to change.' Stephen Covey

## 5.1.6 Positive thinking

Positive thinking is a way of thinking that benefits you and has an immediate positive impact on your life. More specifically, you can think of positive thinking as being a way of thinking that helps you achieve something you want, that helps you feel better and is useful and immediately improves your life.

With these beneficial qualities, positive thinking helps you and serves a practical, useful purpose in your everyday life. The most common reasons for thinking more positively are that it helps make you happier, more confident, and more successful.

### The Formula for Accelerated Change

The overall defining characteristic of positive thinking is that it is useful and immediately improves your life. This distinguishes positive thinking from other types of thinking that are useless and do not improve your life in any way.

To understand this, consider the classic example of looking at a glass, and thinking of it as either half full or half empty. It's neither right nor wrong to look at the glass as either half full or half empty. However, if looking at the glass as half full naturally makes you feel happier, while looking at the glass as half empty naturally makes you feel depressed, then what is the most sensible way of looking at the glass? For this example, if you want to be happy, it makes sense to look at the glass as half full rather than half empty.

After all, this is the more useful, beneficial thing to do, and it is a completely valid and acceptable way of thinking. So, even though it's not 'right', it's clearly a *better* way of thinking about things, no matter which way you look at it.

This example captures the essence of what intelligent positive thinking is all about: identifying acceptable, valid ways of thinking that are useful and beneficial, and, therefore, also very sensible and better in every way.

### What the great leaders say about Positive Thinking:

> 'Being miserable is a habit; being happy is a habit; and the choice is yours.' Tom Hopkins
>
> 'We can complain because rose bushes have thorns, or rejoice because thorn bushes have roses.' Abraham Lincoln
>
> 'Each problem has hidden in it an opportunity so powerful that it literally dwarfs the problem. The greatest success stories were created by people who recognized a problem and turned it into an opportunity.' Joseph Sugarman
>
> 'Man often becomes what he believes himself to be. If I keep on saying to myself that I cannot do a certain thing, it is possible that I may end by really becoming incapable of doing it. On the contrary, if I have the belief that I can do it, I shall surely acquire the capacity to do it even if I may not have it at the beginning.' Mahatma Gandhi
>
> 'Our greatest weakness lies in giving up. The most certain way to succeed is always to try just one more time.' Thomas Edison
>
> 'Hope is a waking dream.' Aristotle

**The Formula for Accelerated Change**

> 'The will to win, the desire to succeed, the urge to reach your full potential… these are the keys that will unlock the door to personal excellence.' Confucius
>
> 'Positive thinking will let you do everything better than negative thinking will' Zig Ziglar
>
> 'Your positive action combined with positive thinking results in success' Shiv Khera
>
> 'You must make a decision that you are going to move on. It won't happen automatically. You will have to rise up and say, 'I don't care how hard this is, I don't care how disappointed I am, I'm not going to let this get the best of me. I'm moving on with my life.' Joel Osteen

### 5.1.7 Creativity

Creativity is a phenomenon whereby something new, and in some way valuable, is created (such as an idea, a joke, a literary work, painting or musical composition, a solution, an invention etc.). Creativity can also be defined 'as the process of producing something that is both original and worthwhile' or 'characterized by originality and expressiveness and imaginative'.

Most people aspire to be creative and to have an original insight which makes them stand out from the crowd. Scientists around the world are exploring what happens in the brain preceding that 'eureka' moment. Their research suggests these five things could help you unleash your creative side.

- Do things differently: If you want to come up with innovative solutions to a problem which is bothering you, then doing something as simple as changing aspects of your daily routine could lead to a creative insight.
- Cut distractions: Another option is to remove all distractions if you wish to try to trigger an epiphany.
- Work on mundane tasks: Another activity to help you trigger your creative brain waves could be to work on something that requires minimal thought.
- Don't be afraid to improvise and take risks.
- Just let your mind wander.

**The Formula for Accelerated Change**

**What the great leaders say about Creativity:**

'An essential aspect of creativity is not being afraid to fail.' Edwin Land

'When all think alike, then no one is thinking.' Walter Lippman

'The chief enemy of creativity is 'good' sense.' Pablo Picasso

'Creativity takes courage.' Henri Matisse

'Creativity is knowing how to hide your sources.' Albert Einstein

'I never made one of my discoveries through the process of rational thinking.' Albert Einstein

'Creativity is contagious, pass it on.' Albert Einstein

'You see things; and you say, 'Why?' But I dream things that never were; and I say, 'Why not?' George Bernard Shaw

'Creativity is just connecting things. When you ask creative people how they did something, they feel a little guilty because they didn't really do it, they just saw something. It seemed obvious to them after a while. That's because they were able to connect experiences they've had and synthesize new things.' Steve Jobs

'In my experience, poor people are the world's greatest entrepreneurs. Every day, they must innovate in order to survive. They remain poor because they do not have the opportunities to turn their creativity into sustainable income.' Muhammad Yunus

'Everybody born comes from the Creator trailing wisps of glory. We come from the Creator with creativity. I think that each one of us is born with creativity.' Maya Angelou

## 5.1.8 Innovation

Innovation is a new idea, device or process. Innovation can be viewed as the application of better solutions that meet new requirements, unarticulated needs, or existing market needs. This is accomplished through more effective products, processes, services, technologies, or ideas that are readily available to markets, governments and society. The term innovation can be defined as something original and more effective and, as a consequence, new, that 'breaks into' the market or society.

## The Formula for Accelerated Change

While a novel device is often described as an innovation, in economics, management science, and other fields of practice and analysis, innovation is generally considered to be a process that brings together various novel ideas in a way that they have an impact on society.

Innovation differs from invention in that innovation refers to the use of a better and, as a result, novel idea or method, whereas invention refers more directly to the creation of the idea or method itself. Innovation differs from improvement in that innovation refers to the notion of doing something different rather than doing the same thing better.

### What the great leaders say about Innovation:

> 'Innovation distinguishes between a leader and a follower.' Steve Jobs
>
> 'Innovation is all about people. Innovation thrives when the population is diverse, accepting and willing to cooperate.' Vivek Wadhwa
>
> 'Innovation is the specific instrument of entrepreneurship. The act that endows resources with a new capacity to create wealth.' Peter Drucker
>
> 'Business has only two functions - marketing and innovation.' Milan Kundera
>
> 'Innovation is the calling card of the future.' Anna Eshoo
>
> 'Invention is not enough. Tesla invented the electric power we use, but he struggled to get it out to people. You have to combine both things: invention and innovation focus, plus the company that can commercialize things and get them to people.' Larry Page

### 5.1.9 New mindset

In decision theory and general systems theory, a mindset is a set of assumptions, methods, or notations held by one or more people or groups of people that is so established that it creates a powerful incentive within those people or groups to continue to adopt or accept prior behaviours, choices, or tools. This phenomenon is also sometimes described as *mental inertia*, 'groupthink', or a 'paradigm', and it is often difficult to counteract its effects upon analysis and decision-making processes.

We all have the ability to change our mindset – to change our core inner beliefs upon which we base our view of ourselves and of the world. But changing our beliefs is not an easy thing to do. Most people find changing one small belief extremely difficult, let alone a whole range of self-supporting

**The Formula for Accelerated Change**

beliefs based on negative pre-conditioning. What is needed is a tool – a tool for change that enables us to rapidly install new thought patterns and positive mindsets, based on proven success models.

Fortunately, our mindset regarding certain aspects of our lives is malleable and is based on the choice of meaning we give to things. If we consciously decide to develop a positive mindset, empowered by positive thinking together with an attitude of joyous expectation of only the best, we put ourselves in the correct frame of mind to propel ourselves into proper action while anticipating and expecting successful outcomes.

**What the great leaders say about on Mindset:**

'Once your mindset changes, everything on the outside will change along with it.'
Steve Maraboli,

'I think anything is possible if you have the mindset and the will and desire to do it and put the time in.' Roger Clemens

'No matter what, people grow. If you chose not to grow, you're staying in a small box with a small mindset. People who win go outside of that box. It's very simple when you look at it.'
Kevin Hart

'My greatest challenge has been to change the mindset of people. Mind sets play strange tricks on us. We see things the way our minds have instructed our eyes to see.' Muhammad Yunus

'Leadership is a mindset that shifts from being a victim to creating results. Any one of us can demonstrate leadership in our work and within our lives' Robin S. Sharma

'Being an entrepreneur is a mindset. You have to see things as opportunities all the time.'
Soledad O'Brien

'If you start with the mindset that you know nothing, you will learn a lot that nobody knew before.' David Moranis

'A creative mindset is in increasingly high demand: employers are vying for workers who are able to dream big and deliver big with the next must-have product. Creative thinking fuels innovation, it leads to new goods and services, creates jobs and delivers substantial economic rewards.' Jim Hunt

'"Never give in" was my mindset.' Arlen Specter

The Formula for Accelerated Change

## 5.1.10 Paradigm shift

A 'paradigm shift' may be thought of as a change from one way of thinking to another. It does not just happen, but rather it is usually driven by agents of change. It can be described as a popular, or perhaps, not so popular shift or transformation of the way we humans perceive events, people, the environment, as well as life itself. It can happen on an individual, national or international scale, and can have a dramatic effect (positive or negative) on the way we live our lives in the present and in the future.

A good example of paradigm shift from 'The Seven Habits of the most effective people of Steven Covey':

> 'Your attitude and behaviour are a function of your paradigm. For example: It's Sunday morning, you are enjoying a quiet ride in the subway – no crowds. A man with several children gets on. The children are rowdy, shouting, disturbing others. You become irritated and finally say "Sir, your children are really disturbing a lot of people, I wonder if you couldn't control them a little more." The reply comes slowly: "I guess I should...We just came from the hospital...Their mother just died about an hour ago and I guess...I don't know what to think...I guess they don't know how to handle it either..." You have just experienced a paradigm shift that puts the situation in a new light. We all see things differently.'

Other examples of paradigm shifts:

> While driving along, a man noticed a woman driving behind him waving her arms and acting kind of oddly. Finally she passed him and shouted out to him 'Pig'. He leaned out of the window and shouted madly 'Sow'. Immediately after that the man hit the pig.

> A bank teller cashed a pay check for a customer. The customer took 3 steps, then stopped, and said, 'Excuse me, I think you made a mistake.' The teller immediately responded 'I'm sorry, but I can't do anything for you. You should have counted it. As soon as you walk away we are no longer responsible.' Whereupon the customer replied, 'Well, okay. Thanks for the extra $20.'

**The Formula for Accelerated Change**

**What the great leaders say about Paradigm shift:**

'He who is good with a hammer tends to think that everything is a nail.' Abraham Maslow

'One never notices what has been done; one can only see what remains to be done.' Marie Curie

'We don't see things as they are, we see things as we are.' Anais Niin

'What we see depends mainly on what we look for.' John Lubbock

'Just because something has always been done in a certain way is never a sufficient reason for continuing to do it that way.' Clarence Birdseye

'The only thing that interferes with my learning is my education.' Albert Einstein

The Formula for Accelerated Change

## 5.2 People

People are individuals, persons or human beings. Each human being has been made by God Almighty for a purpose on earth. The biggest challenge for people is to discover their purpose in life. Without purpose, life has no meaning. People exist to achieve something and it is up to each individual to find his or her own purpose to fulfil and to impact humanity.

To achieve their purpose, people need to equip themselves with various attributes and qualities, such as self-awareness, conscience, dignity, leadership, character, etc.

## 5.2.1 Self-awareness

Self-awareness is the conscious knowledge of one's own character, feelings, motives, and desires. Self-Awareness is having a clear perception of your personality, including your strengths, weaknesses, thoughts, beliefs, motivation, and emotions. Self-awareness allows you to understand other people, how they perceive you, your attitude and your responses to them in the moment.

We might quickly assume that we are self-aware, but it is helpful to have a relative scale for awareness. If you have ever been involved in an auto accident, you may have experienced everything happening in slow motion and noticed details of your thought process and the event. This is a state of heightened awareness. With practice we can learn to engage these types of heightened states and see new opportunities for interpretations in our thoughts, emotions, and conversations.

As you develop self-awareness you are able to make changes in the thoughts and interpretations you make in your mind. Changing the interpretations in your mind allows you to change your emotions. Self-awareness is one of the attributes of Emotional Intelligence and an important factor in achieving success.

Self-awareness is the first step in creating what you want and mastering yourself. Where you focus your attention, your emotions, reactions, personality and behaviour determines where you go in life.

Having self-awareness allows you to see where your thoughts and emotions are taking you. It also allows you to see the controls of your emotions, behaviour, and personality so that you can make the changes you want. Until you are consciously aware of the controls to your thoughts, emotions, words, and behaviour, you will have difficulty making changes in the direction of your life.

### What the great leaders say about on Self-awareness:

'He who knows others is wise. He who knows himself is enlightened.' Lao Tzu

'If I have lost confidence in myself, I have the universe against me.' Ralph Waldo Emerson

Juvenal TURATINZE

**The Formula for Accelerated Change**

---

'I was brought up to believe that how I saw myself was more important than how others saw me.' Anwar el-Sadat

'The most important thing is to be whatever you are without shame.' Rod Steiger

'He that is good for making excuses is seldom good for anything else.' Benjamin Franklin

'No one can give you better advice than yourself.' Cicero

'The only tyrant I accept in this world is the still voice within.' Mahatma Gandhi

'No one can make you feel inferior without your consent.' Eleanor Roosevelt

'We know what we are, but know not what we may become.' William Shakespeare

'Things are not happening to you. Things are happening because of you.' Anonymous

'As human beings, our greatness lies not so much in being able to remake the world ... as in being able to remake ourselves.' Mahatma Gandhi

'A human being is a part of the whole called by us universe; a part limited in time and space. He experiences himself, his thoughts, and his feelings as something separate from the rest — a kind of optical delusion of consciousness.' Albert Einstein

'I think self-awareness is probably the most important thing towards being a champion.' Billie Jean King

'You can't get away from yourself by moving from one place to another.' Ernest Hemingway,

'Man is not what he thinks he is, he is what he hides.' André Malraux'

I am, indeed, a king, because I know how to rule myself.' Pietro Aretino

'The final mystery is oneself.' Oscar Wilde

'Man is least himself when he talks in his own person. Give him a mask, and he will tell you the truth.' Oscar Wilde

---

## 5.2.2 Conscience

Conscience is an aptitude, faculty, intuition or judgment that assists in distinguishing right from wrong. Conscience is an aspect of character that makes moral judgments. Our Character is who we

## The Formula for Accelerated Change

are in the enduring habits of our freedom; our virtues (good character traits) and vices (bad traits). A good conscience requires the development of virtues such as justice, prudence, courage, temperance, faith, hope, and charity. Conscience concentrates all the elements of the person into moral judgments.

In practice, conscience is:

— who we are at the deepest level;
— prudent judgement of actions as compatible with the best of who we are;
— based on objective moral standards;
— always to be followed, if well-formed and certain;
— always a good, when well-formed, even if not always right.

### What the great leaders say about Conscience:

'In matters of conscience, the law of the majority has no place.' Mahatma Gandhi

'You should not believe your conscience and your feelings more than the word which the Lord who receives sinners preaches to you.' Martin Luther

'Our greatest happiness does not depend on the condition of life in which chance has placed us, but is always the result of a good conscience, good health, occupation, and freedom in all just pursuits.' Thomas Jefferson

'I submit that an individual who breaks the law that conscience tells him is unjust and willingly accepts the penalty by staying in jail to arouse the conscience of the community over its injustice, is in reality expressing the very highest respect for law.' Martin Luther King, Jr.

'Never do anything against conscience even if the state demands it.' Albert Einstein

'Justice is a temporary thing that must at last come to an end; but the conscience is eternal and will never die.' Martin Luther

'There is a higher court than courts of justice and that is the court of conscience. It supersedes all other courts.' Mahatma Gandhi

'A clear and innocent conscience fears nothing.' Elizabeth I

'Conscience is a man's compass.' Vincent Van Gogh

'When freedom does not have a purpose, when it does not wish to know anything about the rule of law engraved in the hearts of men and women, when it does not listen to the voice of conscience, it turns against humanity and society.' Pope John Paul II

> 'I cannot and will not recant anything, for to go against conscience is neither right nor safe. Here I stand; I can do no other, so help me God. Amen.' Martin Luther
>
> 'There is a higher law than the law of government. That's the law of conscience.' Stokely Carmichael
>
> 'If a superior give any order to one who is under him which is against that man's conscience, although he do not obey it yet he shall not be dismissed.' St Francis of Assisi
>
> 'A guilty conscience needs to confess. A work of art is a confession.' Albert Camus
>
> 'The human voice can never reach the distance that is covered by the still small voice of conscience.' Mahatma Gandhi
>
> 'The safest course is to do nothing against one's conscience. With this secret, we can enjoy life and have no fear from death.' Voltaire

### 5.2.3 Character

Character is a pattern of behaviour, thoughts and feelings based on universal principles, moral strength, and integrity – plus the guts to live by those principles every day. Character is evidenced by your life's virtues and the 'line you never cross.' Character is the most valuable thing you have, and nobody can ever take it away.

Character in life is what makes people believe in you and is essential both for individual success and for our society to function successfully. Each individual must do his or her part every day by living a life of integrity.

Integrity is adhering to a moral code of honesty, courage, strength and truthfulness – being true to your word. When you don't exhibit integrity, other people get hurt. But you hurt yourself even more.

When you cheat, your 'success' is false. When you break a promise, you are showing that your word is meaningless. When you lie, you deceive others and lose their respect.

Character is the very essence of a particular man. It is indeed what the person is within. It is not liable to change. Character is identity. Character is built by education and cannot change in a short period of time. Virtues that build up good character include courage, patience, fortitude, integrity, honesty, loyalty and good habits. Vices that build up bad character include falsehood, avarice, lust, dishonesty, immodesty and the like.

Your good character is the most important asset you have. It takes a lifetime to build but can be lost in an instant. Once lost, it is difficult to regain. Your true character is revealed when no one else is looking. Often, people decide to act based on short-term gain, or an easy fix to a problem and end up doing the wrong thing.

The old adage 'you are what you do' is true. Failure to consider the long-term consequences of your acts can be disastrous. By studying and focusing on the importance of character, you will be guided by principles, moral strength, and integrity to do the right thing. Nothing is more important for true success in your life.

**The six pillars of character**

**Trustworthiness**

Be honest • Do not deceive, cheat, or steal • Be reliable – do what you say you'll do • Have the courage to do the right thing • Build a good reputation • Be loyal — stand by your family, friends, and country.

**Respect**

Treat others with respect; follow the Golden Rule • Be tolerant and accept differences • Use good manners, not bad language • Be considerate of the feelings of others • Don't threaten, hit or hurt anyone • Deal peacefully with anger, insults, and disagreements.

**Responsibility**

Do what you are supposed to do • Plan ahead • Persevere: keep on trying! • Always do your best • Use self-control • Be self-disciplined • Think before you act – consider the consequences • Be accountable for your words, actions, and attitudes • Set a good example for others.

**Fairness**

Play by the rules • Take turns and share • Be open-minded; listen to others • Don't take advantage of others • Don't blame others carelessly • Treat all people fairly.

**Caring**

Be kind • Be compassionate and show you care • Express gratitude • Forgive others • Help people in need.

**The Formula for Accelerated Change**

## Citizenship

Do your share to make your community better • Cooperate • Get involved in community affairs • Stay informed; vote • Be a good neighbour • Obey laws and rules • Respect authority • Protect the environment • Volunteer.

### What the great leaders say about Character:

> 'The function of education is to teach one to think intensively and to think critically… Intelligence plus character – that is the goal of true education.' Martin Luther King, Jr.
>
> 'A good character carries with it the highest power of causing a thing to be believed.' Aristotle
>
> 'A man's character is his fate.' Heraclitus
>
> Character is destiny.' Heraclitus
>
> 'The best index to a person's character is (a) how he treats people who can't do him any good, and (b) how he treats people who can't fight back.' Abigail Van Buren
>
> 'Nearly all men can stand adversity, but if you want to test a man's character, give him power.' Abraham Lincoln
>
> 'Character is power.' Booker T. Washington
>
> 'Character is like a tree and reputation is like its shadow. The shadow is what we think of it; the tree is the real thing.' Abraham Lincoln
>
> 'Character is, in the long run, the decisive factor in the life of individuals and of nations alike.' Theodore Roosevelt
>
> 'Characters do not change. Opinions alter, but characters are only developed.' Benjamin Disraeli

## 5.2.4 Attitude

Attitude is the opinion or the method by which one approaches a given situation. Attitude is built by experience. Attitude is a firm opinion about something. Attitude is liable to change according to the situation. It is after all a kind of surface emotion. Attitude represents an individual's degree of likes or dislikes for a given thing or a given situation. Attitude can change in a short period of time.

## The Formula for Accelerated Change

You have a choice in the way you perceive whatever is going on. You have the power to choose whether you think the glass is half full or half empty.

A positive attitude does not pop into your mind by itself. How you feel is a decision you make every day. If you don't automatically feel upbeat, look around and find something to feel good about. Aim: Start out each day in a positive way.

Nothing can stop the person with the right mental attitude from achieving his/her goal. Nothing on earth can help the person with the wrong mental attitude.

We are beings of perception, and the quality of our perception is determined by our attitude. This is the importance of attitude.

An individual who has openness, honesty, and subtlety to perceive the nuances of his/her attitude in each moment, and the concentration necessary to make corrections as necessary is truly an unlimited person. For it is our attitude that determines the reality we live in and the opportunities and experiences we are available for.

Two individuals can be out in the pouring rain with one having the time of his/her life, while the other is soaked, cold, and in short, miserable. The difference is not in the environment, but in their perception of the environment. And that is where attitude comes in.

If we can pay attention to our attitude and become aware enough to identify the nuances of our attitudes, then we can discover the limitations of our beliefs, thoughts, and emotional states which may have become so habitual that we may not even notice their detrimental effects and the ways in which they limit us.

Changing our attitude is not an event but a continuous process, like everything related to self-mastery and evolution. You don't need to change everything at once. Instead just make whatever attitudinal shifts are relevant to you in your daily life and reinforce them consistently until they become your new attitude. And as you do this you will find yourself naturally moving on to new areas, and new levels of subtlety.

### What the great leaders say about Attitudes:

> 'Your *attitude*, not your aptitude, will determine your *altitude*.' Zig Ziglar
>
> 'Nothing can stop the man with the right mental attitude from achieving his goal; nothing on earth can help the man with the wrong mental attitude.' W. W. Ziege
>
> 'The greatest discovery of any generation is that a human being can alter his life by altering his attitude.' William James

Juvenal TURATINZE

## The Formula for Accelerated Change

'A positive attitude causes a chain reaction of positive thoughts, events and outcomes. It is a catalyst and it sparks extraordinary results.' Wade Boggs

'The greatest discovery of all time is that a person can change his future by merely changing his attitude.' Oprah Winfrey

'Everything can be taken from a man or a woman but one thing: the last of human freedoms –to choose one's attitude in any given set of circumstances, to choose one's own way.' Victor Frankl

'Nothing in life is to be feared, it is only to be understood. Now is the time to understand more, so that we may fear less.' Marie Curie

'No one can make you feel inferior without your consent.' Eleanor Roosevelt

'In order to be big, you have to think big. If you think small, you're going to be small.' Emeril Lagasse

'Attitudes are contagious. Are yours worth catching?' Dennis and Wendy Mannering

'Oh, my friend, it's not what they take away from you that counts. It's what you do with what you have left.' Hubert Humphrey

'Attitude is a little thing that makes a big difference.' Winston Churchill

'Happiness is an attitude. We either make ourselves miserable, or happy and strong. The amount of work is the same.' Francesca Reigler

'If you don't like something, change it. If you can't change it, change your attitude.' Maya Angelou

'You must start with a positive attitude or you will surely end without one.' Carrie Latet

'If you have the will to win, you have achieved half your success; if you don't, you have achieved half your failure.' David Ambrose

'Watch your thoughts, for they become words.
Choose your words, for they become actions.
Understand your actions, for they become habits.
Study your habits, for they will become your character.
Develop your character, for it becomes your destiny.
It's not what you get in life. It's what YOU do with it!'
The 'Original' Mike Smith

Juvenal TURATINZE

**The Formula for Accelerated Change**

## 5.2.5 Beliefs and values

The clearer you are about what you value and believe in, the happier and more effective you will be.

**Beliefs** are the assumptions we make about ourselves, about others in the world and about how we expect things to be. Beliefs are about how we think things really are, what we think is really true and what therefore expect are likely consequences that will follow from our behaviour. Beliefs are valuable resources, generalizations that people use to give themselves a sense of certainty and a basis for decision-making in an uncertain and ambiguous world.

We tend not to question our beliefs because we are so certain about them and many of them stem from childhood. Our beliefs can be changed or turned round by the 'reprogramming' of our subconscious.

Our **values** are things that we deem important and can include concepts like equality, honesty, education, effort, perseverance, loyalty, faithfulness etc. Our values are very much individual and they affect us at a deep subconscious level. Every decision we make is based on our values and either we use them as avoidance or for aspiration. Values are about how we have learnt to think things ought to be or people ought to behave, especially in terms of qualities such as honesty, integrity and openness.

Many of the limitations you face in life are self-imposed. What you believe about yourself can keep you locked behind your fears or thrust you forward into living your dreams.

You become what you believe you are. Think of yourself as a work in progress. Actually, we all are. Identify old limiting beliefs that may be holding you back and get rid of them.

**What the great leaders say about Beliefs and values:**

'Our beliefs about what we are and what we can be precisely determine what we can be.'
Anthony Robbins

'Beliefs have the power to create and the power to destroy. Human beings have the awesome ability to take any experience of their lives and create a meaning that disempowers them or one that can literally save their lives.' Tony Robbins

'Your beliefs become your thoughts,
Your thoughts become your words,
Your words become your actions,

Juvenal TURATINZE

**The Formula for Accelerated Change**

Your actions become your habits,
Your habits become your values,
Your values become your destiny.'
Mahatma Gandhi

'If you don't change your beliefs, your life will be like this forever. Is that good news?'
W. Somerset Maugham

'Find people who share your values and you'll conquer the world together.' John Ratzenberger

'It's not hard to make decisions when you know what your values are.' Roy Disney

'Don't waste your love on somebody, who doesn't value it.' William Shakespeare, *Romeo and Juliet*

'When your values are clear to you, making decisions becomes easier.' Roy Disney

'Never compromise your values.' Steve Maraboli

'A people that values its privileges above its principles soon loses both.' Dwight D. Eisenhower

'Nowadays people know the price of everything and the value of nothing.' Oscar Wilde

'Nothing can have value without being an object of utility.' Karl Marx

'Price is what you pay. Value is what you get.' Warren Buffett

## 5.2.6 Self-discipline

No personal success, achievement, or goal, can be realised without self-discipline. It is singularly the most important attribute needed to achieve any type of personal excellence or outstanding performance.

Self-discipline is the ability to control one's impulses, emotions, desires and behaviour. It is being able to turn down immediate pleasure and instant gratification in favour of gaining the long-term satisfaction and fulfilment from achieving higher and more meaningful goals. Dr Myles Munroe defines self-discipline as self-imposed standards for the sake of a higher goal.

Self-discipline is one of the important ingredients of success. It expresses itself in a variety of ways:

- perseverance;
- the ability not to give up, despite failure and setbacks;
- self control;

## The Formula for Accelerated Change

- the ability to resist distractions or temptations;
- trying over and again, until you accomplish what you set out to do.

To possess self-discipline is to be able to make the decisions, take the actions, and execute your game plan regardless of the obstacles, discomfort, or difficulties that may come your way.

Certainly, being disciplined does not mean living a limiting or a restrictive lifestyle. Nor, does it mean giving up everything you enjoy or relinquishing fun and relaxation. It does mean learning how to focus your mind and energies on your goals and persevere until they are accomplished. It also means cultivating a mindset whereby you are ruled by your deliberate choices rather than by your emotions, bad habits, or the sway of others. Self-discipline allows you to reach your goals in a reasonable time frame and to live a more orderly and satisfying life.

Building self-discipline starts by making the decision to go forward and learning what it takes to get there. Learn what motivates you and what your bad triggers are. Get rid of some of your bad and self-defeating habits. Avoid distractions and focus on what is important to you. Learn to say no to some of your feelings, impulses and urges. Train yourself to do what you know to be right, even if you don't feel like doing it. Stop and think before you act. Think about consequences. When you practice self-restraint it helps you develop the habit of keeping other things under control.

If we are to be masters of our own destiny, we must develop self-discipline and self-control. By focusing on long-term benefits instead of short-term discomfort, we can encourage ourselves to develop self-discipline.

### What the great leaders say about Self-Discipline:

'Vision determines discipline.' Dr Myles Munroe

'The first and best victory is to conquer self.' Plato

'You can never conquer the mountain. You can only conquer yourself.' Jim Whittaker

'You can never conquer the mountain. You can only conquer yourself.' Jim Whittaker

'A man without decision of character can never be said to belong to himself … He belongs to whatever can make captive of him.' John Foster

'I think the guys who are really controlling their emotions ... are going to win.' Tiger Woods

We are what we repeatedly do, excellence then is not an act, but a habit.' Aristotle

**The Formula for Accelerated Change**

---

'Nothing is more harmful to the service, than the neglect of discipline; for that discipline, more than numbers, gives one army superiority over another.' George Washington

'If we don't discipline ourselves, the world will do it for us.' William Feather

'Mastering others is strength. Mastering yourself is true power.' Lao Tzu

'Self-discipline is a form of freedom. Freedom from laziness and lethargy, freedom from the expectations and demands of others, freedom from weakness and fear - and doubt. Self-discipline allows a pitcher to feel his individuality, his inner strength, his talent. He is master of, rather than a slave to, his thoughts and emotions.' H.A. Dorfman

'A disciplined mind leads to happiness, and an undisciplined mind leads to suffering.' Dalai Lama

'Discipline is the bridge between goals and accomplishment.' Jim Rohn

'Discipline is the soul of an army. It makes small numbers formidable; procures success to the weak, and esteem to all.' George Washington

'We need to understand the difference between discipline and punishment. Punishment is what you do to someone; discipline is what you do for someone.' Zig Ziglar

---

## 5.2.7 Dignity

Dignity is the inherent value and worth of human beings; everyone is born with it. Dignity has to do with the way people feel, think and behave in relation to the worth or value of themselves and others. To treat someone with dignity is to treat them as being of worth, in a way that is respectful of them as a valued individual.

Dignity is a person's right to be treated like a human being. When we talk about human dignity, we mean human rights. If people are treated with dignity, they usually have the right to make choices for themselves. Dignity also means that people are treated with respect. When we talk about the dignity of the elderly, for example, we mean treating them like adults and not like children. Ultimately, dignity is the idea that human beings are different from animals.

Dignity is something that a person has within him or herself. People cannot give you dignity (though they can treat you as if you have it). Instead, dignity can only, ultimately, come from within.

### The Formula for Accelerated Change

Dignity is when you act as if you matter. It is when you act as if you respect yourself. It does not mean that you do whatever you want or that you act in selfish ways. It means that you act as if you care about yourself and about your character.

Dignity is a concept that focuses on the worth, nobility, and importance of the individual. You show your understanding of other people's dignity by honouring them (e.g. paying attention to what they like and asking them) and by respecting them (e.g. treating them with fairness, justice, compassion). You show your understanding of your own dignity by acting according to your sense of importance, worth, value, and of having a noble nature (e.g. having high aspirations, conducting yourself admirably, valuing your abilities and ideas, and acting so as to further good end results).

### What the great leaders say about Dignity:

'Any man or institution that tries to rob me of my dignity will lose.' Nelson Mandela

'A wise man has dignity without pride; a fool has pride without dignity.' Conficius

'The basic tenet of black consciousness is that the black man must reject all value systems that seek to make him a foreigner in the country of his birth and reduce his basic human dignity.' Steven Biko

'Dignity does not consist in possessing honours, but in the consciousness that we deserve them.' Aristotle

'There are two kinds of pride, both good and bad. 'Good pride' represents our dignity and self-respect. 'Bad pride' is the deadly sin of superiority that reeks of conceit and arrogance.' John C. Maxwell

'All labour that uplifts humanity has dignity and importance and should be undertaken with painstaking excellence.' Martin Luther King, Jr.

'One's dignity may be assaulted, vandalized and cruelly mocked, but it can never be taken away unless it is surrendered.' Michael J. Fox

'Politeness [is] a sign of dignity, not subservience.' Theodore Roosevelt

'Without dignity, identity is erased.' Laura Hillenbrand

'Human rights rest on human dignity. The dignity of man is an ideal worth fighting for and worth dying for.' Robert Maynard

**The Formula for Accelerated Change**

'I believe in human dignity as the source of national purpose, human liberty as the source of national action, the human heart as the source of national compassion, and in the human mind as the source of our invention and our ideas.' John Fitzgerald Kennedy

### 5.2.8 Leadership

People are born to lead and make change happen. For changes to happen people with effective and visionary leadership are needed. 'Everything rises and falls on leadership,' says Dr John C. Maxwell. Leadership is about change. Change is created by leaders who have decided to become change agents.

Leadership is about influencing others to work towards a vision. To influence other people, a person needs to have a vision they believe in and be willing to transfer it to them. A good leader is someone who is able to share and transfer their vision to other people who take on that vision and become followers. A great and visionary leader transforms their followers into leaders in their own right. The great leader imparts their followers to become leaders in the areas of their talents and gifting. The leadership success happens when the followers become successful leaders.

Successful leadership requires strong belief in the vision, a good character, a clear conscience, an open mind, good qualities, developed competencies and readiness to serve others. The prime function of a leader is to serve other people. A true leader is satisfied by the success of others.

As a human being, you are born with leadership potential. You are created as a potential leader and you have the capacity to influence others. But to become a visionary leader, you have to discover your vision, your talent, and your passion. You also need to improve your knowledge, competences and skills in a specific area of your leadership. To make an impact as a leader, it is very important that you develop a strong will to act, serve others and make sacrifices for them. Leadership is about acting, making progress and transforming lives. Leaders act to make changes by doing things differently but positively. Leadership must lead a change that translates into human betterment.

All great leaders, like Jesus Christ, Mahatma Gandhi, Martin Luther King Jr. and Nelson Mandela have the following in common:

- they have lived to serve others and sacrificed for them;
- they had a powerful and clear vision;
- before starting to influence others, they improved themselves, they studied and equipped themselves with sufficient knowledge and strong beliefs;
- they trained others and made them leaders who continued the work when they died;
- they acted, worked hard without seeking reward from anybody for what they did.

## The Formula for Accelerated Change

Here are some steps to develop your leadership:

- analyse yourself critically and find out who you are and how you think;
- know your attitude, your talent, your beliefs and your aptitude and make a plan to improve them.

### What the great leaders say about Leadership:

'My philosophy is, trapped in every follower is a leader. My belief is, if that person is placed in the right environment, the leader will manifest herself or himself.' Dr Myles Munroe

'If the blind lead the blind, both shall fall in the ditch.' Jesus Christ

'You were born to lead but you must become a leader.' Dr Myles Monroe

'The purpose for true leadership is the production of leaders.' Dr Myles Monroe

'Leadership success is measured by the success of your successor.' Dr Myles Monroe

'Men make history and not the other way around. In periods where there is no leadership, society stands still. Progress occurs when courageous, skilful leaders seize the opportunity to change things for the better.' Harry Truman

'All Leadership is influence.' John C. Maxwell

'Management is efficiency in climbing the ladder of success; leadership determines whether the ladder is leaning against the right wall.' Stephen R. Covey

'It is no use walking anywhere to preach unless our walking is our preaching.' St. Francis of Assisi

'The led must not be compelled; they must be able to choose their own leader.' Albert Einstein

'Nearly all men can stand adversity, but if you want to test a man's character, give him power.' Abraham Lincoln

'The function of leadership is to produce more leaders, not more followers.' Ralph Nader

'A leader is a dealer in hope.' Napoleon Bonaparte

'To be able to lead others, a man must be willing to go forward alone.' Harry Truman

'If your actions inspire others to dream more, learn more, do more and become more, you are a leader.' John Quincy Adams

Juvenal TURATINZE

**The Formula for Accelerated Change**

'The growth and development of people is the highest calling of leadership.' Harvey S. Firestone

'Leadership is about change... The best way to get people to venture into unknown terrain is to make it desirable by taking them there in their imaginations.' Noel Tichy

'Leadership development is a lifetime journey, not a quick trip.' John Maxwell

'A leader is best when people barely know he exists, not so good when people obey and acclaim him, worst when they despise him. But of a good leader, who talks little, when his work is done, his aim fulfilled, they will say, 'We did this ourselves.' Lao-Tse

'The first responsibility of a leader is to define reality. The last is to say thank you. In between, the leader is a servant.' Max DePree

'The most dangerous leadership myth is that leaders are born – that there is a genetic factor to leadership. This myth asserts that people simply either have certain charismatic qualities or not. That's nonsense; in fact, the opposite is true. Leaders are made rather than born.' Warren Bennis

'The very essence of leadership is that you have to have a vision.' Theodore Hesburgh

'A leader takes people where they want to go. A great leader takes people where they don't necessarily want to go, but ought to be.' Rosalynn Carter

'Leaders are more powerful role models when they learn than when they teach.' Rosabeth Moss Kantor

'Good leaders must first become good servants. 'Robert Greenleaf

'I start with the premise that the function of leadership is to produce more leaders, not more followers.' Ralph Naber

'I suppose leadership at one time meant muscles; but today it means getting along with people.' Mahatma Gandhi

'The key to successful leadership today is influence, not authority.' Kenneth Blanchard

'How do you know you have won? When the energy is coming the other way and when your people are visibly growing individually and as a group.' Sir John Harvey-Jones

## The Formula for Accelerated Change

> 'Speak softly and carry a big stick; you will go far.' Theodore Roosevelt
>
> 'The final test of a leader is that he leaves behind him in other men, the conviction and the will to carry on.' Walter Lippmann
>
> 'In a different world we need to find a niche for ourselves, little corners where in spite of our small size we can perform a role which will be useful to the world. To do that, you will need people at the top, decision-makers who have got foresight, good minds, who are open to ideas, who can seize opportunities like we did... My job really was to find my successors. I found them, they are there; their job is to find their successors. So there must be this continuous renewal of talented, dedicated, honest, able people who will do things not for themselves but for their people and for their country. If they can do that, they will carry on for another one generation and so it goes on. The moment that breaks, it's gone.' Lee Kuan Yew, Prime Minister of Singapore (1959-1990)

In a few words, **LEADERSHIP** is:

**L**ead by Example
**E**ncourage the Heart
**A**ppreciate Diversity
**D**evelop People's Potential
**E**nable and Empower
**R**ealist
**S**erve
**H**elp/Coach Where Necessary
**I**nspire a Shared Vision
**P**rocess Challenge

## Leadership Characteristics - Top Ten List:

1. Visionary
2. Integrity
3. Consistency
4. Coach/Facilitator
5. Accessibility
6. Flexibility
7. Courage
8. Over-Communicates

Juvenal TURATINZE

**The Formula for Accelerated Change**

9. Positive Role Model
10. Inspirational

## 5.2.9 Learning

Learning is the act of acquiring new, or modifying and reinforcing; existing knowledge, behaviours, skills, values, or preferences and may involve synthesising different types of information. Learning is a process, rather than a collection of factual and procedural knowledge. Learning produces changes in the individual and the changes produced are relatively permanent. Human learning may occur as part of education, personal development, schooling, or training.

Learning is also a measurable and relatively permanent change in behaviour through experience, instruction, or study. Whereas individual learning is selective, group learning is essentially political its outcomes depend largely on power playing in the group. Learning itself cannot be measured, but its results can be.

Life is a learning process and learning is a lifelong process.

Lifelong learning is one of the most effective ways of dealing with change, and change is constant – change in our personal lives, change in our work lives, change in our local communities, governance, associations and organisations, etc. One of the most influential management writers, Peter Drucker, wrote: 'We now accept the fact that learning is a lifelong process of keeping abreast of change. And the most pressing task is to teach people how to learn.'

**What the great leaders say about Learning:**

'Once you stop learning, you start dying.' Albert Einstein

'We now accept the fact that learning is a lifelong process of keeping abreast of change. And the most pressing task is to teach people how to learn.' Peter Drucker

'The beautiful thing about learning is that nobody can take it away from you.' B. B. King

'An investment in knowledge always pays the best interest.' Benjamin Franklin

'I hear and I forget. I see and I remember. I do and I understand.' Chinese proverb

'A single conversation with a wise man is better than ten years of study.' Chinese proverb

'Tell me and I forget. Teach me and I remember. Involve me and I learn.' Benjamin Franklin

'I never learned from a man who agreed with me.' Robert A. Heinlein

# The Formula for Accelerated Change

'Live as if you were to die tomorrow. Learn as if you were to live forever.' Mahatma Gandhi

'Education is what remains after one has forgotten what one has learned in school.' Albert Einstein

'Any fool can know. The point is to understand.' Albert Einstein

'For the things we have to learn before we can do them, we learn by doing them.' Aristotle

'It is not that I'm so smart. But I stay with the questions much longer.' Albert Einstein

'The more I read, the more I acquire, the more certain I am that I know nothing.' Voltaire

'Leadership and learning are indispensable to each other.' John F. Kennedy

'There is no school equal to a decent home and no teacher equal to a virtuous parent.'
Mahatma Gandhi

'The expert knows more and more about less and less until he knows everything about nothing.'
Mahatma Gandhi

'Learning never exhausts the mind.' Leonardo da Vinci

'We must learn to live together as brothers or perish together as fools.' Martin Luther King, Jr.

'There is no end to education. It is not that you read a book, pass an examination, and finish with education. The whole of life, from the moment you are born to the moment you die, is a process of learning.' Jiddu Krishnamurti

'I am always doing that which I cannot do, in order that I may learn how to do it.' Pablo Picasso

'You cannot open a book without learning something.' Confucius

'I like to listen. I have learned a great deal from listening carefully. Most people never listen.'
Ernest Hemingway

'If history repeats itself, and the unexpected always happens, how incapable must Man be of learning from experience?' George Bernard Shaw

'The secret of success is learning how to use pain and pleasure instead of having pain and pleasure use you. If you do that, you're in control of your life. If you don't, life controls you.' Tony Robbins

'Your most unhappy customers are your greatest source of learning.' Bill Gates

**The Formula for Accelerated Change**

> If we knew what it was we were doing, it would not be called research, would it? Albert Einstein
>
> 'I am always ready to learn although I do not always like being taught.' Winston Churchill
>
> 'I am a woman in process. I'm just trying like everybody else. I try to take every conflict, every experience, and learn from it. Life is never dull.' Oprah Winfrey
>
> 'Being ignorant is not so much a shame, as being unwilling to learn.' Benjamin Franklin
>
> 'I have never met a man so ignorant that I couldn't learn something from him.' Galileo Galilei
>
> 'We are the creative force of our life, and through our own decisions rather than our conditions, if we carefully learn to do certain things, we can accomplish those goals.' Stephen Covey
>
> 'All I have learned, I learned from books.' Abraham Lincoln
>
> 'Anyone who stops learning is old, whether at twenty or eighty. Anyone who keeps learning stays young. The greatest thing in life is to keep your mind young.' Henry Ford

## 5.2.10 Empowerment and Mentoring

Empowerment is about having or taking more control over all aspects of your life.

On an individual level we see empowerment as building confidence, insight and understanding, and developing personal skills, for example, being able to analyse situations and communicate more effectively with others. Being empowered presupposes some level of common sense and emotional maturity and access to appropriate information and know-how; it also implies someone who cares about others and is tolerant of other's views and behaviours (within limits!).

Within a group or community, empowerment can be taken to involve building trust, cooperation and communication between members, and a prerequisite for this is that there are appropriate structures, protocols and procedures in place, with effective sanctions against those who default or abuse the system. There must be opportunities for people to meet and exchange views and opinions, and ways of recording what is agreed upon and done; and there must be scope for having fun and celebrating achievement.

Empowerment is about recognising that people already have power through their knowledge, experience and motivation, and then creating an environment that encourages letting that power out.

**The Formula for Accelerated Change**

Empowerment comes as people contribute their full potential in attaining both personal and collective objectives. Your role as an empowering leader might be considered as this: To create conditions in which other people can contribute their maximum potential capacity to achieve the strategic goals and desired results.

**What the great leaders say about Empowerment:**

'As we look ahead into the next century, leaders will be those who empower others.' Bill Gates

'Education is not a tool for development – individual, community and the nation. It is the foundation for our future. It is empowerment to make choices and emboldens youth to chase their dreams.'
Nita Ambani

### 5.2.11 Team building

Team building is a process that develops cooperation and teamwork within a group of people to reach a common goal. To constitute an effective team, its members must trust each other, have respect for each other, and be motivated to use the strengths of each member to achieve their objectives.

It takes great leadership to build great teams. It takes leaders who are not afraid to correct their course, make difficult decisions and establish standards of performance that are constantly being met – and improving at all times. Whether in the workplace, professional sports, or your local community, team building requires a keen understanding of people, their strengths and what gets them excited to work with others. Team building requires the management of egos and their constant demands for attention and recognition. Team building is both an art and a science, and the leader who can consistently build high performance teams is a great leader.

To lead a team effectively, a leader must first establish his leadership with each team member. The most effective team leaders build their relationships with trust and loyalty, rather than with fear or the power of their positions.

Getting it right at the beginning greatly increases the chances that your team will not only work well together, but most important of all that it delivers on the task it was set to do. To do that, make sure you have these five critical components of the ideal team in place:

**Set a clear goal.** A common sense of purpose unites team members and provides a context within which they can understand the functioning of the team and how their own contributions play a part.

## The Formula for Accelerated Change

The goal must contain challenge, appeal to personal pride, and provide an opportunity to make a difference and know it. Then the goal can become a powerful vision.

**Build organisational support.** Teams are always more productive when they have the clear support of the organisation and access to the resources to support their efforts. Get that clear from the outset.

**Create a team structure that empowers team members.** Create shared expectations, identify and organise resources; work on how all the team does its work in the best possible way.

**Identify key relationships.**
Build key relationships with individuals, other teams and the whole organisation to allow the very best access to the resources you need for your team.

**Monitor external factors.** Gathering and analysing information about the external environment that is relevant to your team's goals enables it to make adjustments quickly as necessary possibly pre-empting problems before they begin.

**One more thing.** When a team stops working well together it is often because team members have no common vision, have different and conflicting ideas about what the team's mission is and what they are expected to deliver. Don't forget that effective teams begin and end with a clear vision and purpose.

A team's purpose doesn't spell out how the team will carry out its work, but it does explain what the end result is supposed to be. Get these basics in place and you have the formula for building highly successful teams.

### What the great leaders say about Team building:

'Alone we can do so little; together we can do so much.' Helen Keller

'Remember teamwork begins by building trust. And the only way to do that is to overcome our need for invulnerability.' Patrick Lencioni

'Coming together is a beginning. Keeping together is progress. Working together is success.' Henry Ford

## The Formula for Accelerated Change

'Talent wins games, but teamwork and intelligence win championships.' Michael Jordan

'Teamwork is the ability to work together toward a common vision. The ability to direct individual accomplishments toward organizational objectives. It is the fuel that allows common people to attain uncommon results.' Andrew Carnegie

'No man is wise enough by himself.' Plautus

'Interdependent people combine their own efforts with the efforts of others to achieve their greatest success.' Stephen Covey

'Individual commitment to a group effort – that is what makes a team work, a company work, a society work, a civilization work.' Vince Lombardi

'Build for your team a feeling of oneness, of dependence on one another and of strength to be derived by unity.' Vince Lombardi

'T.E.A.M = Together Everyone Achieves More.' Anonymous

'We = power' Lorii Myers,

'Great team can accomplish great works.' Lailah Gifty Akita,

'Individual commitment to a group effort – that is what makes a team work, a company work, a society work, a civilization work.' Vince Lombardi

'Teamwork makes the dream work, but a vision becomes a nightmare when the leader has a big dream and a bad team.' John C. Maxwell

'I'm lucky to be part of a team who help to make me look good, and they deserve as much of the credit for my success as I do for the hard work we have all put in on the training ground.' Lionel Messi

'The bottom line is, when people are crystal clear about the most important priorities of the organization and team they work with and prioritized their work around those top priorities, not only are they many times more productive, they discover they have the time they need to have a whole life.' Stephen Covey

**The Formula for Accelerated Change**

### 5.2.12 Empathy

Empathy is the capacity to understand what another person is experiencing from within the other person's frame of reference, i.e. the capacity to place oneself in another's shoes. It is the ability to sense other people's emotions, coupled with the ability to imagine what someone else might be thinking or feeling.

Empathy is an important skill to practice. It will lead to greater personal and professional successes and will allow you to become happier the more you practice.

Developing an empathetic approach is perhaps the most significant effort you can make toward improving your people skills. When you understand others, they'll probably want to understand you; and this is how you can start to build cooperation, collaboration, and teamwork.

To be empathetic, you have to think beyond yourself and your own concerns. Once you see beyond your own world, you'll realise that there's so much to discover and appreciate.

People who are accused of being egoistical and selfish, or lacking perspective, have often missed the big picture: that they are only one person in a world with billions of other people.

To start using empathy more effectively, consider the following:

1. **Put aside your viewpoint, and try to see things from the other person's point of view.**

   When you do this, you'll realise that other people most likely aren't being evil, unkind, stubborn, or unreasonable – they're probably just reacting to the situation with the knowledge they have.

2. **Validate the other person's perspective.**

   Once you 'see' why others believe what they believe, acknowledge it. Remember: acknowledgement does not always equal agreement. You can accept that people have different opinions from your own, and that they may have good reasons to hold those opinions.

3. **Examine your attitude.**

   Are you more concerned with getting your way, winning, or being right? Or, is your priority to find a solution, build relationships, and accept others? Without an open mind and attitude, you probably won't have enough room for empathy.

**The Formula for Accelerated Change**

### 4. Listen.

Listen to the entire message that the other person is trying to communicate.

- o Listen with your ears – what is being said, and what tone is being used?
- o Listen with your eyes – what is the person doing with his or her body while speaking?
- o Listen with your instincts – do you sense that the person is not communicating something important?
- o Listen with your heart – what do you think the other person feels?
- o

### 5. Ask what the other person would do.

When in doubt, ask the person to explain his or her position. This is probably the simplest, and most direct way to understand the other person. However, it's probably the least used way to develop empathy.

Practice these skills when you interact with people. You'll likely appear much more caring and approachable – simply because you increase your interest in what others think, feel, and experience. It's a great gift to be willing and able to see the world from a variety of perspectives – and it's a gift that you can use all of the time, in any situation.

**What the great leaders say about Empathy:**

'Empathy is about standing in someone else's shoes, feeling with his or her heart, seeing with his or her eyes. Not only is empathy hard to outsource and automate, but it makes the world a better place.'
Daniel H. Pink

'I call him religious who understands the suffering of others.' Mahatma Gandhi

'No one cares how much you know, until they know how much you care.' Theodore Roosevelt

'I do not ask the wounded person how he feels; I myself become the wounded person.'
Walt Whitman

'Leadership is about empathy. It is about having the ability to relate to and connect with people for the purpose of inspiring and empowering their lives.' Oprah Winfrey

'The great gift of human beings is that we have the power of empathy, we can all sense a mysterious connection to each other.' Meryl Streep

**The Formula for Accelerated Change**

---

'When you show deep empathy toward others, their defensive energy goes down, and positive energy replaces it. That's when you can get more creative in solving problems.' Stephen Covey

'My third piece of advice is to cultivate a sense of empathy – to put yourself in other people's shoes – to see the world from their eyes. Empathy is a quality of character that can change the world.'
Barack Obama

'A person with Ubuntu is open and available to others, affirming of others, does not feel threatened that others are able and good, based from a proper self-assurance that comes from knowing that he or she belongs in a greater whole and is diminished when others are humiliated or diminished, when others are tortured or oppressed.' Desmond Tutu

'You know when ubuntu is there, and it is obvious when it is absent. It has to do with what it means to be truly human, to know that you are bound up with others in the bundle of life.' Desmond Tutu

'If there is any one secret of success, it lies in the ability to get the other person's point of view and see things from his angle as well as your own.' Henry Ford

---

## 5.2.13 Dialogue

One of the most effective team-building tools of leaders is the ability to build dialogue skills. In times of fast change, learning to leverage the enormous benefits of different perspectives is essential. But, building a diverse team only brings benefit if these differences can lead to a broader, richer perspective. Dialogue, a very different way of communicating and benefiting from differences, can be an essential path toward achieving this goal.

Dialogue is the opposite of debate, or verbal 'fight,' the goal of which is to win an argument by besting an opponent. The focus is on listening for flaws in the 'opponent's' argument rather than listening to understand something new or from a different perspective. Ego is typically at the centre of this win-lose conversation.

Dialogue is also different from discussion, the 'breaking apart' of issues, individuals or situations to gain agreement. Discussions tend to be fast-paced, persuasive conversations in which one person tries to convince the other of a point of view or solution. Ego, control and power over others are often at the forefront of this style of talking.

Dialogue is a communication skill essential to achieving a consensus decision. It is based on the idea that the IQ of the team can, potentially, be much higher than the IQ of individuals. What keeps our thinking about an issue at a lower level is worrying about 'defending' our position rather than attempting to explore meaning from another person's viewpoint. The purpose of dialogue is to go

## The Formula for Accelerated Change

beyond any one individual's understanding. Dialogue is reserved for complex, difficult issues when there are no easy answers.

### What the great leaders say about Dialogue:

'Change happens by listening and then starting a dialogue with the people who are doing something you don't believe is right.' Jane Goodall

'Behind every argument is someone's ignorance.' Louis D. Brandeis

'Listening, not imitation, may be the sincerest form of flattery.' Dr Joyce Brothers

'They may forget what you said, but they will never forget how you made them feel.'
Carl W. Buechner

'The only way to get the best of an argument is to avoid it.' Dale Carnegie

'When dealing with people, remember you are not dealing with creatures of logic, but creatures of emotion.' Dale Carnegie

'Courage is what it takes to stand up and speak; courage is also what it takes to sit down and listen.'
Winston Churchill

'The reality today is that we are all interdependent and have to co-exist on this small planet. Therefore, the only sensible and intelligent way of resolving differences and clashes of interests, whether between individuals or nations, is through dialogue.' The Dalai Lama

'Dialogue and education for peace can help free our hearts from the impulse toward intolerance and the rejection of others.' Daisaku Ikeda

'The best way to solve problems and to fight against war is through dialogue.' Malala Yousafzai

'Dialogue between people of differing views is critical for fostering understanding in a democracy.'
Alex Gibney

## 5.2.14 Synergy

Stephen Covey said that 'Synergy is what happens when one plus one equals ten or a hundred or even a thousand! It's the profound result when two or more respectful human beings determine to go beyond their preconceived ideas to meet a great challenge.'

## The Formula for Accelerated Change

Synergy is the benefit that results from the efforts of two or more agents who work together to achieve something that one couldn't have achieved on his own. It's the concept of the whole being greater than the sum of its parts. Synergy requires union where people come together despite differences. Marriage is the union of husband and wife.

Synergy is the creation of a whole that is greater than the simple sum of its parts.

A synergistic working relationship is a powerful phenomenon to witness in action—people working together to consume the fewest resources possible to get the job done, while achieving a higher quantity and quality output than if they worked independently.

### What the great leaders say about Synergy:

'The whole is greater than the sum of its parts.' Aristotle

'Synergy is better than my way or your way. It's our way.' Stephen Covey

'Synergy is the creation of a whole that is greater than the sum of its parts.' Ray French

'Nobody can achieve success alone.' Ifeanyi Enoch Onuoha

'Alone we can do so little; together we can do so much.' Helen Keller

'Synergy: The combined effect of individuals in collaboration that exceeds the sum of their individual effects.' Stephen Covey

'When mutual understanding and respect are present, the spirit of synergy inevitable starts to develop.' Stephen Covey

'The greatest benefit of synergy is born in the diversity of perspectives. The highest value can be found in these variances. Too much of the same does not create change in the same way.' Danielle Marie Crune

'Synergy between thoughts and feelings reads the universe like an opened book.' Tony Beta

## 5.2.15 Critical mass

The critical mass of people is the minimum number of people required to start or sustain an operation, business, process, etc. A critical mass is a sufficient number of adopters of an innovation

### The Formula for Accelerated Change

in a social system so that the rate of adoption becomes self-sustaining and creates further growth. The term is borrowed from nuclear physics and in that field it refers to the amount of a substance needed to start a chain reaction.

A critical mass for change is the minimum number of people needed to start a chain of change or multiple changes. When this minimum number is attained, the change will start to happen among people exponentially. The initiators and adopters will influence a number of people equal or higher to their number squared.

Relationship systems change by reaching critical mass. The idea of a critical tipping point in people and relationships works if you think of change as growth. Critical mass for change ('tipping point') can also be 'a point of no return'.

In social science the term critical mass is widely used to refer to any context in which things change after a certain number of people get together or enter a setting. Social movement activists and scholars often use 'critical mass' in a loose metaphorical way to refer to an initial group of protesters or actors that is big enough to accomplish social change.

Critical mass is achieved in changing processes when 'the people and systems operating in the new way achieve unstoppable momentum.' The key word here is 'people', for it is the behavioural or people component of change that is the most challenging.

Achieving critical mass is a key part of building momentum and making change stick. Without it, stakeholders will likely revert back to the way things were done before the change was introduced and there is a risk of not being able to sustain the change. Creating a common vision and supporting people to take actions and achieve it is the way to embed change and achieve a sense of critical mass. A critical mass of people becomes a guiding coalition that leads and drives change.

A critical mass that sustains change is achieved in three phases: Mobilisation, Implementation and Solidification.

Before you can even achieve a critical mass, you need to build the case for change and mobilise the effort in the first phase. In the **Mobilisation** phase, stakeholders must believe that the change benefits outweigh the risks involved, the vision is attainable, the leader is trustworthy and the processes are reliable.

As a leader you need to be able to acknowledge the losses that people may be feeling and adapt your communication to address the concerns of people. Frequent communication, whether formally or informally, will encourage mobilisation towards the desired future state.

The next phase is **Implementation**. This is where the old and the new systems are competing for survival. People will feel a range of emotions from anger, resentment, and resignation to relief and excitement. It is important to continue explaining the vision, create temporary structures as necessary to encourage the new behaviour, and encourage people to think of new ways to do things as well as take risks. It is in this phase that people push hard for critical mass. Once critical mass has been achieved, the last phase, **Solidification**, accelerates the change and solidifies the new state by essentially removing the old approach. Align your support with change makes it easier for you to lead it.

**What the great leaders say about Critical mass:**

> 'When an idea reaches critical mass there is no stopping the shift its presence will induce.'
> Marianne Williamson

## 5.2.16 Movement

Movements are about mobilising people behind a shared purpose. They can start out with just a small group of people who believe passionately in something and they can end up changing the culture around the world.

Movements, the kind that gather around positive, creative, dynamic ideas can help build a better, fairer, more sustainable and more interesting world.

To make a significant impact, an idea needs to become a movement. It needs to inspire others to rally behind it and push it forward. Starting a movement can be a never-ending cycle that just keeps turning.

Building a movement of change follows the **theory[8] of diffusion of innovations** that seeks to explain how, why, and at what rate new ideas and technology spread through cultures.

---

[8] The theory of diffusion of innovations has been developed by Everett Rogers in his book *Diffusion of Innovations*

## The Formula for Accelerated Change

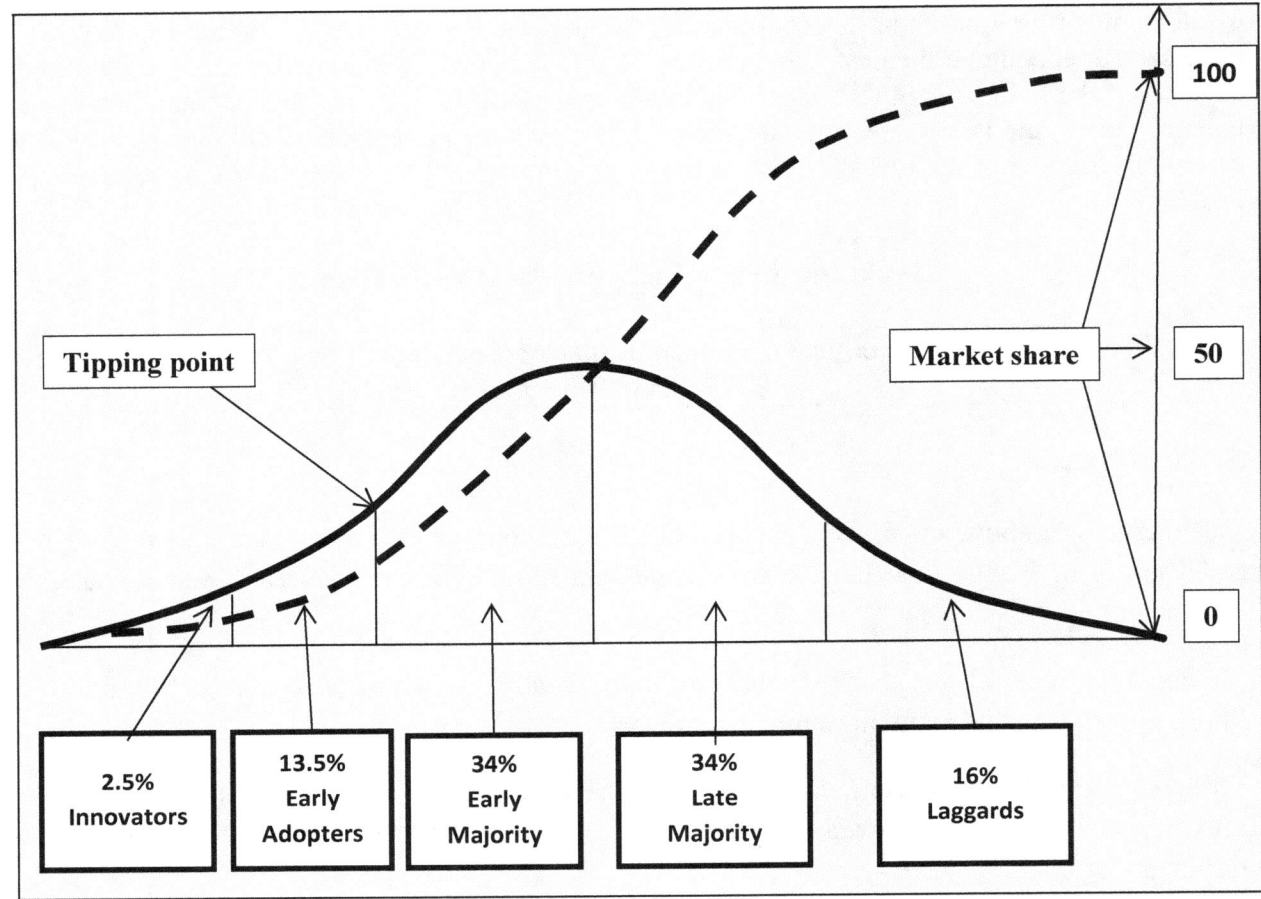

Figure 1: The diffusion of innovations

With successive groups of consumers adopting the new technology, its market share (curve) will eventually reach the saturation level. In mathematics, the bright curve is known as the logistic function. The curve is broken into sections of adopters. The theory is that each category of adopters acts as an influencer and reference group for the next.

The law of diffusion of innovation shows that the adoption curve (a typical bell curve) can be segmented out into the following sections.

Of all the population:

1. 2.5% innovators
2. 13.5% early adopters

---

published in 1962.

Juvenal TURATINZE

## The Formula for Accelerated Change

3. 34% early majority
4. 34% late majority
5. 16% laggards

The Formula for Accelerated Change follows the same law and here of all the population:

1. 2.5% visionaries
2. 13.5% leaders
3. 34% early majority followers
4. 34% late majority followers
5. 16% laggards or sceptics

From a personal vision, **a visionary**, or **i**nitiator or **innovator** comes with an idea, and others will follow, as described here:

- **Visionaries** (2.5%) are the people with the same vision as the visionary who join him/her quickly;
- **Leaders (**13.5%) are people who believe in what the visionaries believe in and join as soon as possible;
- **Early majority followers** (34%) are people who will wait to see the first results and follow when they are convinced that new ideas are working and can produce the desired change;
- **Late majority followers** (34%) are the people with doubt and fear risks. They join when they are completely sure to gain the benefits;
- **Laggards** (16%) are sceptical people who will join only when there is no other option left for them.

It is important for visionaries and leaders to be able to understand and identify how movements are created. This will enable them to reach the tipping point quicker when looking to create change.

People's movements of change are about building leaders, trust and sustainable organisations that can win. The raw materials of movements are leadership, trust, campaigns and a certain sense of moral solidarity. The focus of a movement is solving a deep-rooted problem.

**The Formula for Accelerated Change**

Movement-building requires three big parts:

1. Organising for big change – we're talking about transformational change, not just winning a single campaign.
2. Bringing new people on board – our first instinct when organising is to first start with people we know we share the same beliefs and vision with. To bring new and diverse people on board, we must take a step further and engage in deep listening and collaboration with other people and organisations.
3. Ensuring a sustainable movement through trust, commitment and leadership – movements that succeed are ones that last years. Building trust, commitment –and especially leadership – from the ground up, is critical.

Here are five quick ideas on helping propel a movement forward:

1. Find a cause and a vision with a connection to people's deepest passions and beliefs about right and wrong, a cause that makes them think about what really matters, about creating a better world for their children.
2. Identify concrete actions that will push the movement forward.
3. Set concrete targets, a schedule and an end date by which to accomplish the actions.
4. Enlist partners who share the passion and vision and ensure that the movement is not about any individual or organisation. The cause has to be so important that individual and group identities can be temporarily put aside in pursuit of the goal.
5. Measure progress toward the goal and be relentless in using data to push the movement forward.

The greatest social movements have taught us that with enough determination and commitment, extraordinary things can happen. All of us share a responsibility to act in the face of inequality, poverty, and injustice. If we don't act, nothing changes, injustice persists, and poverty becomes more entrenched. It is possible to build a movement to end poverty and enhance shared prosperity that will change the world, even in these difficult times. We can make it happen.

### What the great leaders say about on Social movements:

'The great thing about social movements is everybody gets to be a part of them.' Jim Wallis

'As I review the great history of our nation, community organizers have been at the center of so many of our great social movements.' Cory Booker

'A social movement that only moves people is merely a revolt. A movement that changes both people and institutions is a revolution.' Martin Luther King Jr.

Juvenal TURATINZE

**The Formula for Accelerated Change**

'A critical element in nearly all effective social movements is leadership. For it is through smart, persistent, and authoritative leaders that a movement generates the appropriate concepts and language that captures the frustration, anger, or fear of the group's members and places responsibility where it is warranted.' David E. Wilkins

**The Formula for Accelerated Change**

## 5.3 Actions

It is by actions that vision is translated into reality. Action is something done with a purpose. Actions make change happens. But actions have to be driven by a vision and a sense of purpose.

**What the great leaders say about Actions:**

'It looks impossible until it is done.' Nelson Mandela

'Vision without action is merely a dream. Action without vision just passes the time. Vision with action can change the world.' Joel A. Barker

'Infuse your life with action. Don't wait for it to happen. Make it happen. Make your own future. Make your own hope. Make your own love. And whatever your beliefs honour your creator, not by passively waiting for grace to come down from upon high, but by doing what you can to make grace happen... yourself, right now, right down here on earth.' Bradley Whitford

'In order to carry a positive action we must develop here a positive vision.' Dalai Lama

'If your actions inspire others to dream more, learn more, do more and become more, you are a leader.' John Quincy Adams

'Great thoughts speak only to the thoughtful mind, but great actions speak to all mankind.' Theodore Roosevelt

'Thinking is easy, acting is difficult, and to put one's thoughts into action is the most difficult thing in the world.' Johann Wolfgang von Goethe

'Patriotism is voluntary. It is a feeling of loyalty and allegiance that is the result of knowledge and belief. A patriot shows their patriotism through their actions, by their choice.' Jesse Ventura

'Leadership is practiced not so much in words as in attitude and in actions.' Harold S. Geneen

'In essence, if we want to direct our lives, we must take control of our consistent actions. It's not what we do once in a while that shapes our lives, but what we do consistently,' Tony Robbins

'Leaders are responsible not for running public opinion polls but for the consequences of their action.' Henry A. Kissinger

'We become just by performing just action, temperate by performing temperate actions, brave by performing brave action.' Aristotle

**The Formula for Accelerated Change**

## 5.3.1 Independent will

Independent will is the ability to keep the promises we make to ourselves and others. It is the ability to make decisions and choices and to act in accordance with those choices and decisions. The extent to which our independent will is developed is tested in our day-to-day lives in the form of personal integrity. It is the ability to give meaning to our words and walk the walk. It is an integral part of how much value is placed on oneself.

**What the great leaders say about on Independent will:**

'Independent will is our capacity to act. It gives us the power to transcend our paradigms, to swim upstream, to rewrite our scripts, to act based on principle rather than reacting based on emotion or circumstance.' Stephen Covey

## 5.3.2 Responsibility

Responsibility is a duty, obligation or liability for which someone is held accountable.

Being responsible refers to our ability and our independent will to make decisions and take the necessary actions to provide the right response that serves our own interests and the interests of others. We first need to be responsible for ourselves before we can be responsible for others.

Every human being has responsibility. People are held accountable for the actions they perform whether helpful or harmful.

The real meaning of responsibility is the ability to respond. It's going out and creating what you want through personal choices. The responsibility that each of us has is that we are completely, 100% responsible for how our lives turn out. Being responsible involves having some skills, a caring and open attitude, and a good sense of what we can and cannot do.

Responsibility means ownership: owning what needs doing and accepting blame when we cause problems. Responsibility also means committing ourselves – to lead, to create, to solve problems and then following through. It involves taking risks and working hard.

Rights and responsibilities are two sides of the same coin; when we have power or resources, we have responsibility to use them well. It is important to be aware of where our responsibilities end and where the responsibilities of other begin.

### The Formula for Accelerated Change

### What the great leaders say about Responsibility:

'Nobody can do it for you.' Ralph Cordiner

'Every right implies a responsibility; every opportunity, an obligation, Every possession, a duty.' John D. Rockefeller

'One's philosophy is not best expressed in words; it is expressed in the choices one makes... and the choices we make are ultimately our responsibility.' Eleanor Roosevelt

'Rank does not confer privilege or give power. It imposes responsibility.' Peter Drucker

'We are made wise not by the recollection of our past, but by the responsibility for our future.' George Bernard Shaw

'In dreams begin responsibilities.' W.B. Yeats

'Liberty means responsibility. That is why most men dread it.' George Bernard Shaw,

'Accept responsibility for your life. Know that it is you who will get you where you want to go, no one else.' Les Brown

'Accountability breeds response-ability.' Stephen Covey

'All business depends upon men fulfilling their responsibilities.' Mahatma Gandhi

'Faced with crisis, the man of character falls back on himself. He imposes his own stamp of action, takes responsibility for it, makes it his own.' Charles de Gaulle

'The key is taking responsibility and initiative, deciding what your life is about and prioritizing your life around the most important things.' Stephen Covey

'I recommend that the Statue of Liberty be supplemented by a Statue of Responsibility on the west coast.' Viktor E. Frankl

'No alibi will save you from accepting the responsibility.' Napoleon Hill

'Responsibility walks hand in hand with capacity and power.' Josiah Gilbert Holland

**The Formula for Accelerated Change**

---

'Unto whomsoever much is given, of him shall much be required.' [Luke 12:48] Bible

'You cannot escape the responsibility of tomorrow by evading it today.' Abraham Lincoln

'Whatever happens, take responsibility.' Anthony Robbins

'You might well remember that nothing can bring you success but yourself.' Napoleon Hill

---

## 5.3.3 Initiative

Initiative is the power or ability to begin or to follow through energetically with a plan or task; enterprise and determination.

### What the great leaders say about Initiative:

---

'The best way to not feel hopeless is to get up and do something. Don't wait for good things to happen to you. If you go out and make some good things happen, you will fill the world with hope, you will fill yourself with hope.' — Barack Obama

'Do not wait for leaders; do it alone, person to person.' Mother Teresa

'Success comes from taking the initiative and following up... persisting... eloquently expressing the depth of your love. What simple action could you take today to produce a new momentum toward success in your life?' Tony Robbins

'Without initiative, leaders are simply workers in leadership positions.' Bo Bennett

'Initiative is doing the right thing without being told.' Victor Hugo

'Time is neutral and does not change things. With courage and initiative, leaders change things.' Jesse Jackson

'Never relinquish the initiative.' Charles de Gaulle

'I am personally convinced that one person can be a change catalyst, a 'transformer' in any situation, any organization. Such an individual is yeast that can leaven an entire loaf. It requires vision, initiative, patience, respect, persistence, courage, and faith to be a transforming leader.' Stephen Covey

---

### 5.3.4 Action Planning

Action planning is a process which will help you focus on your ideas and to decide what steps you need to take to achieve the particular goals that you may have. It is a statement of what you want to achieve over a given period of time. Preparing an action plan is a good way to help you reach your objectives in life.

It involves:

- identifying your objectives to reach your vision;
- setting objectives which are achievable measurable;
- prioritising your tasks effectively;
- identifying the steps needed to achieve your goals;
- being able to work effectively under pressure;
- completing work to a deadline;
- having a contingency plan or plan B.

An effective action plan should give you a concrete timetable and a set of clearly defined steps to help you reach your objective, rather than aimlessly wondering what to do next. It helps you to focus on your ideas and provides you with an answer to the question 'what do I do to achieve my objective?'.

The main steps in preparing an action plan are as follows:

- **Have a vision.** (Why should I do this?). What are the reasons for my actions? What problems do I want to solve? It is important to have a clear picture of the desired future situation.
- **Have a clear objective.** ('Where do I want to be?'). To be motivating a goal needs to be challenging enough to stimulate, but not so difficult as to be demoralising. It should be just outside your comfort zone: stretching but not highly stressful. Be precise about what you want to achieve.
- **List the benefits you would gain by achieving your goal.**

- **Start with what you will do now.** There is no point in having an action plan that will start in six months' time.

- **Define clearly the steps you will take.** ('How do I get there?') Think of all the possible things you could do that would take you closer to achieving your goal, no matter how small. Break down any large steps into smaller components, so it doesn't seem so difficult to achieve. What is the biggest obstacle? What could go wrong?

**The Formula for Accelerated Change**

- **Identify the end point for each step and** give yourself a small **reward** for achieving it.

- **Arrange the steps in a logical, chronological order and put a date by which you will start each step.** Put these dates into your diary or onto a calendar. Try to set yourself weekly goals: what research you will do into jobs, what skills you will concentrate on learning etc. It's also a good idea to get into the habit of planning a timetable each evening listing your tasks for the next day or two.

**What the great leaders say about Action planning:**

'By failing to plan, you are planning to fail.' Benjamin Franklin

'A journey of a thousand miles begins with a single step.' Lao Tzu

'Success is the sum of small efforts, repeated day-in and day-out.' Robert Collier

'Never confuse motion with action.' Benjamin Franklin.

'Unless you have a definite, precise, clearly set goal, you are not going to realize the maximum potential that lies within you.' Zig Ziglar

'Well begun is half done.' Mary Poppins

'One of the advantages of being disorganized is that one is always having surprising discoveries.' Winnie the Pooh

## 5.3.5 Proactivity

**Proactivity** or Proactive behaviour involves acting in advance of a future situation, rather than just reacting. It means taking control and making things happen rather than just adjusting to a situation or waiting for something to happen. Proactive people do not wait for things to happen to them, they anticipate and act to take control over circumstances. They focus on what they can and what they can influence. Being proactive is about taking responsibility for your life.

The proactive individual has a **vision**. They create meaning in life by striving for ambitious goals. Again, these need not necessarily be socially desirable goals. Missionaries, politicians, entrepreneurs, teachers, or athletes may have dreams that conflict with those of others, but they have dreams. They have an imagination of what could be, and they set goals in line with their vision. They accumulate resources, prevent resource depletion, and mobilise forces with a long-term aim in mind. They have a mission, imposed by themselves.

### The Formula for Accelerated Change

The proactive individual is driven by **values**. The behaviours of others might be determined by their social environment, whereas proactive persons are, in contrast, mindful of their values and choose their path of action accordingly. Although values are influenced by others during the socialisation process, people differ in the degree to which their life depends on these values. Once the socially mediated values are internalised they become the leading force to guide the proactive individual's endeavours.

The proactive individual takes **responsibility** for his or her own growth. A life course is not fully determined by external forces but can be chosen. Neither good nor bad events are mindlessly attributed to external causes. Rather, the proactive individual faces reality and adopts a balanced view of self-blame and other-blame in the case of negative events. However, two kinds of responsibilities have to be distinguished: Responsibility for past events and responsibility for making things happen. The latter is the crucial one here. The proactive individual focuses on solutions for problems, irrespective of whether the problems have been caused by him or herself or by others.

Proactive Attitude is a personality characteristic which pushes people to be **motivated** and to take **action**.

### What the great leaders say about Proactivity:

'The way to bring about change is to be proactive and active.' Octavia Spencer

'A leadership culture is one where everyone thinks like an owner, a CEO or a managing director. It's one where everyone is entrepreneurial and proactive.' Robin S. Sharma

'Everyone must be proactive and do all they can to help themselves to stay employed.' Stephen Covey

'People are always blaming their circumstances for what they are. I don't believe in circumstances. The people who get on in this world are the people who get up and look for the circumstances they want, and if they can't find them, make them.' George Bernard Shaw

'Learn from yesterday, live for today, hope for tomorrow. The important thing is not to stop questioning.' Albert Einstein

'The weaker mind reacts.' Toba Beta

'You can overcome your circumstances or you can let your circumstances overcome you.' Richie Norton,

## The Formula for Accelerated Change

'Happiness is a choice. Happiness does not depend on outward conditions but on inward decisions.' Cameron C. Taylor,

'People who end up with the good jobs are the proactive ones who are solutions to problems, not problems themselves, who seize the initiative to do whatever is necessary, consistent with correct principles, to get the job done.' Stephen Covey,

'Remember, action today can prevent a crisis tomorrow.' Steve Shallenberger,

'I believe that everyone chooses how to approach life. If you're proactive, you focus on *preparing*. If you're reactive, you end up focusing on *repairing*.' John C. Maxwell,

'Do what today others won't, so tomorrow, you can do what others can't.' Brian Rogers Loop –

'A wise person does at once, what a fool does at last. Both do the same thing; only at different times.' Unknown

'Whatever you want to do, do it now! There are only so many tomorrows.' Pope Paul VI

'The beginning is the most important part of the work.' Plato

## 5.3.6 Prioritising

Someone who works hard and is well organised but spends all his/her time on unimportant tasks may be efficient but not effective. Efficiency and effectiveness are not the same. To be effective, you need to decide what tasks are urgent and important and to focus on these. This is called prioritising. It's important to list the tasks you have and to sort these in order of priority, and then to devote most time to the most important tasks. This avoids the natural tendency to concentrate on the simple, easy tasks and to allow too many interruptions to your work. Differentiate also between urgent and important tasks: an urgent task may not necessarily be important!

### What the great leaders say about Prioritising:

'The key is not to prioritize what's on your schedule, but to schedule your priorities.'
Stephen Covey

**The Formula for Accelerated Change**

---

'You have to decide what your highest priorities are and have the courage – pleasantly, smilingly, non-apologetically, to say "no" to other things. And the way you do that is by having a bigger "yes" burning inside. The enemy of the "best" is often the "good".' Stephen Covey

'Action expresses priorities.' Mahatma Gandhi

'Most of us spend too much time on what is urgent and not enough time on what is important.' Stephen Covey

'Begin each day with God. It will change your priorities.' Elizabeth George

---

### 5.3.7 Organising

'Organisation is the process of identifying and grouping the works to be performed, defining and delegating responsibility and authority and establishing relationships for the purpose of enabling people to work most efficiently.' Louis A. Allen

### Importance of Organising

- Organising helps Organisations to reap the benefit of specialisation.
- Organising provides for Optimum utilisation of resources.
- Organising helps in Effective administration.
- Organising channels for Expansion and growth.
- Organising achieves coordination among different departments.
- Organising creates scope for new change.

### What the great leaders say about Organising:

---

'Successful organizing is based on the recognition that people get organized because they, too, have a vision.' Paul Wellstone

'The key to organizing an alternative society is to organize people around what they can do, and more importantly, what they want to do.' Abbie Hoffman

'Organize, don't agonize.' Nancy Pelosi

'Organizing is what you do before you do something, so that when you do it, it is not all mixed up.' A.A. Milne

'Three Rules of Work: Out of clutter find simplicity; From discord find harmony; In the middle of difficulty lies opportunity.' Albert Einstein

---

**The Formula for Accelerated Change**

---

'If you want to live a happy life, tie it to a goal, not to people or things.' Albert Einstein

'For every minute spent organizing, an hour is earned.' Benjamin Franklin

'You will never be completely ready. Start from wherever you are.' C.J. Hayden, MCC

---

### 5.3.8 Speaking

Speaking is the most effective way of communication. Leaders share their vision by speaking to others. The legendary leaders spoke and transmitted their messages through teaching, speeches, conversations, dialogue, etc. Jesus is known to be the best teacher; he spent his time teaching people, mainly his disciples. Martin Luther King Jr. was a great orator; he is remembered for his speeches. His 'I have a dream' speech is said to be the best speech of the 20th century. Mahatma Gandhi spoke to spread his messages; his quotes are known to have universal wisdom.

Speaking is an important act for any person to serve and lead people; it is why speaking skills are important for development as a leader. It is not about clever phrasing or brilliant rhetoric. The best leadership is expressed through simple and clear language: language that the audience understands, addressing the issues the audience cares about. In fact, what great leaders do is speak to the concerns of their audiences. That means knowing what those concerns are at that moment in time and framing them for the audience in a way that is understandable, memorable and actionable.

Speaking and influencing people for change is done in four steps:

- Tell them **why:** why things are the way they are and why they should be changed; why things need to be different; why it matters; and most importantly, why they matter in all of this. Share the vision.
- Tell them **how:** how things should be changed and how things will be. Give a plan.
- Tell them **what:** what actions need to be done to change the situation of things. Tell what to do immediately.
- Tell them **who:** the 'who' who is going to act and change things is not anybody else but the people present themselves. Use 'you' to speak directly to the people who are listening. Tell them 'it is up to you to do everything necessary'.

**What the great leaders say about Speaking:**

---

'You can speak well if your tongue can deliver the message of your heart.' John Ford

'Wise men speak because they have something to say; Fools because they have to say something.'
Plato

---

## The Formula for Accelerated Change

'There are always three speeches, for every one you actually gave. The one you practiced, the one you gave, and the one you wish you gave.' Dale Carnegie

'It usually takes me more than three weeks to prepare a good impromptu speech.' Mark Twain

'Be sincere, be brief; be seated.' Franklin D. Roosevelt

'If you have nothing to say, say nothing.' Mark Twain

'Listen to many, speak to a few.' William Shakespeare

'Courage is what it takes to stand up and speak; courage is also what it takes to sit down and listen.' Winston Churchill

'Think twice before you speak, because your words and influence will plant the seed of either success or failure in the mind of another.' Napoleon Hill

'A good speech should be like a woman's skirt; long enough to cover the subject and short enough to create interest.' Winston S. Churchill

'Men of few words are the best men.' William Shakespeare

'When angry count to ten before you speak. If very angry, count to one hundred.' Thomas Jefferson

'Do you wish people to think well of you? Don't speak well of yourself.' Blaise Pascal

'Speak ill of no man, but speak all the good you know of everybody.' Benjamin Franklin

'I know all about audiences, they believe everything you say, except when you are telling the truth.' Mark Twain

### 5.3.9 Entrepreneurship

Entrepreneurship is the capacity and willingness to develop, organise and manage a business venture along with any of its risks in order to make a profit. The most obvious example of entrepreneurship is starting new businesses.

In economics, entrepreneurship combined with land, labour, natural resources and capital can produce profit. An entrepreneurial spirit is characterised by innovation and risk-taking, and is an

**The Formula for Accelerated Change**

essential part of a nation's ability to succeed in an ever-changing and increasingly competitive global marketplace.

More recently, the term entrepreneurship has been extended to include a specific mindset resulting in entrepreneurial initiatives, e.g. in the form of social entrepreneurship, political entrepreneurship, or knowledge entrepreneurship.

An entrepreneur is a person who develops a new idea and takes the risk of setting up an enterprise to produce a product or service which satisfies customer needs. All entrepreneurs are business persons, but not all business persons are entrepreneurs. Entrepreneurs are the business people who are not satisfied with their performance and therefore always find ways to improve and grow.

Here are the characteristics or some special qualities and strengths which make entrepreneurs different from business people. It is important for us to note that successful entrepreneurs possess the following characteristics.

### Initiative

Entrepreneurs take actions that go beyond job requirements or the demand of the situation. They create ideas that bring about phenomenal changes.

### Opportunity seeking

Entrepreneurs are quick to see and seize opportunities. They do things before they are asked to work by people or forced by situations.

### Persistence

Entrepreneurs are not discouraged by the difficulties and problems that come up in their business or their personal life. Once they set a goal and are committed to it, they will become completely absorbed in it.

### Information seeking

Entrepreneurs undertake personal research on how to satisfy customers and solve problems. They know that different people have different capabilities that can be of help to them. They seek out the relevant information from their clients, suppliers, competitors and others. They always want to learn things which will help the business grow.

Juvenal TURATINZE

## The Formula for Accelerated Change

### Demand for quality and efficiency

Entrepreneurs are always competing with others to do things better, faster, and at less cost. They strive to achieve excellence.

### Risk taking

Are you afraid of uncertainties? Then you cannot be an entrepreneur. Entrepreneurs are not high risk-takers. Nor are they gamblers; they calculate their risks before taking action. They place themselves in situations involving moderate risk, so they are moderate risk-takers.

### Goal setting

Entrepreneurs set meaningful and challenging goals for themselves. Entrepreneurs do not just dream. They think and plan about what they do. They are certain or have hope about the future.

### Commitment to work

Entrepreneurs will work long hours to be able to keep their promise to clients. They do the work together with their workers to get a job done. They know how to make the people who work for them happy due to their dynamic leadership.

### Systematic planning and monitoring

Entrepreneurs plan for whatever they expect in the business. They do not leave things to chance. They plan by breaking large tasks down into small ones and set time limits against them. Since an entrepreneur knows what to expect at any time, they are able to change plans and strategies to achieve what they aim at.

### Persuasion and networking

Entrepreneurs acts to develop and maintain business contacts by establishing good working relationships. They use deliberate strategies to influence others.

### Independence and self confidence

Most entrepreneurs start a business because they like to be their own bosses. They are responsible for their own decisions.

**The Formula for Accelerated Change**

**What the great leaders say about Entrepreneurship:**

'Innovation is the specific instrument of entrepreneurship. The act that endows resources with a new capacity to create wealth.' Peter Drucker

'What is great about entrepreneurship is that entrepreneurs create the tangible from the intangible.' Robert Herjavec

'Entrepreneurship, entrepreneurship, entrepreneurship. It drives everything: Job creation, poverty alleviation, innovation.' Elliott Bisnow

'I'm convinced that about half of what separates the successful entrepreneurs from the non-successful ones is pure perseverance.' Steve Jobs

'It's not about ideas. It's about making ideas happen.' Scott Belsky

'The secret to successful hiring is this: look for the people who want to change the world.' Marc Benioff

'When everything seems to be going against you, remember that the airplane takes off against the wind, not with it.' Henry Ford

'If you're not a risk taker, you should get the hell out of business.' Ray Kroc

'Watch, listen, and learn. You can't know it all yourself. Anyone who thinks they do is destined for mediocrity.' Donald Trump

'Always deliver more than expected.' Larry Page

'A person who never made a mistake never tried anything new.' Albert Einstein

'The way to get started is to quit talking and begin doing.' Walt Disney

'Do not be embarrassed by your failures, learn from them and start again.' Richard Branson

'It does not matter how slowly you go as long as you do not stop.' Confucius.

'Your most unhappy customers are your greatest source of learning.' Bill Gates

'I have not failed. I've just found 10,000 ways that won't work.' Thomas Edison

'Entrepreneurship is neither a science nor an art. It is a practice.' Peter Drucker

**The Formula for Accelerated Change**

## 5.4 Time

Everything can change; it is a only matter of time!

Time is the most precious thing in life. It influences every single moment and everything we do. To manage time is to manage life! Time is free, but it's priceless. You can't own it, but you can use it. You can't keep it, but you can spend it. Once you've lost it you can never get it back.

Time is more valuable than money. You can get more money, but you cannot get more time. Be it a president or a street trader, everybody has 24 hours in a day. Every day, hour, minute, second is precious for us. Time is managed like money. In the same way that we spend money wisely: so too we should spend our time very cautiously. For this time management is very essential.

A successful man only knows the value of time because he has come up with the proper use of time with hard work. So, time should not be procrastinated instead every single second should be used carefully.

The use of your time determines who you are and who you will become, and that is why time management is a very important element for your success. Achieving the change you want will depend on how best you use time. Change can happen quickly, later or never happen depending on how you use your time.

**What the great leaders say about Time:**

---

'Time is money.' Benjamin Franklin

'Time is a created thing. To say "I don't have time" is to say "I don't want to".' Lao Tzu

'My favourite things in life don't cost any money. It's really clear that the most precious resource we all have is time.' Steve Jobs

'The only reason for time is so that everything doesn't happen at once.' Albert Einstein

'Lost time is never found again.' Benjamin Franklin

'We must use time wisely and forever realize that the time is always ripe to do right.' Nelson Mandela

'In all our deeds, the proper value and respect for time determines success or failure.' Malcolm X

'Don't wait. The time will never be just right.' Napoleon Hill

---

**The Formula for Accelerated Change**

> 'Our greatest weakness lies in giving up. The most certain way to succeed is always to try just one more time.' Thomas Edison
>
> 'Do you love life? Then don't waste time, because time is life!' Benjamin Franklin

## 5.4.1 Time management

Time management is the act or process of planning and exercising conscious control over the amount of time spent on specific activities, especially to increase effectiveness, efficiency or productivity.

The aim of managing your time is to spend time doing the things that help you achieve your goals and the things that you personally prioritise and value.

Time management is about effective scheduling of your time, goal setting, prioritising and choosing what to do and what not to do, delegating tasks, analysing and reviewing your spent time, organising your workspace, keeping your concentration and focus on your work, motivating yourself to work towards a goal.

Time management is important because it is the number one skill you need to learn if you want to become successful. Without time management, you give yourself over to coincidence. You won't steer your life and you'll eventually do what others want you to do. If you study and practice time management, you take your life into your own hands. You are in control and you decide where you want to go to.

## The Eisenhower Method of Time Management

The Eisenhower Method helps you decide which action you should or shouldn't undertake. It helps you to divide actions into one of four categories. The quadrants are divided by importance and urgency.

> *'What is important is seldom urgent and what is urgent is seldom important.'*
> - Dwight D. Eisenhower

## Who was Eisenhower?

He was the American general (he later became president of the US) who commanded the D-Day landings in Normandy to free France from the Germans in the Second World War. He commanded 2 million soldiers and was forced to find a better way to control them. He then came up with the Eisenhower method.

**The Formula for Accelerated Change**

### How to Use the Eisenhower Method

Using the Eisenhower quadrant is very easy. You pick an item from your to-do-list and you ask yourself these two questions.

*'Is it urgent?' and 'Is it important?'*

You can now put the action into the correct quadrant. Below is an explanation of each quadrant.

| | Urgent | Not Urgent |
|---|---|---|
| **Important** | **I**<br>**Fire Fighting**<br>Crises<br>Pressing problems<br>Deadline-driven projects | **II**<br>**Quality Time**<br>Prevention, capacity improvement<br>Relationship building<br>Recognising new opportunities<br>Planning, recreation |
| **Not Important** | **III**<br>**Distraction**<br>Interruptions, some callers<br>Some mails, some reports<br>Some meetings, pressing matters<br>Popular and social activities | **IV**<br>**Time Wasting**<br>Busy work, some mail<br>Some phone calls<br>Time wasters<br>Pleasant activities |

Figure 2: Time management quadrant

### 1) Urgent and Important

You have to do these actions. They're important. They progress you toward your goals, however, since they're urgent, they're often unplanned and unwanted.

You will always spend some time here, since emergencies will always happen. When they do, you have to deal with them. No excuses. After you dealt with the situation, spend time to make sure it never happens again or minimise its occurrence or make preparations for when it happens again. For example, When cooking, make sure you have all the ingredients before you start, because you don't want to be running to the shop to buy some salt when you're in the middle of cooking.

**The Formula for Accelerated Change**

## 2) Not Urgent and Important

This is the quadrant in which you should spent most of your time. Most people however, don't do this and spend most of their time in any of the other quadrants. Because these important tasks don't scream at you like a ringing phone, they're often neglected in favour of more urgent matters.

If you spend almost no time here, then your first important task is to save some time each day to work on the important things. One thing you can do is to set up systems to avoid tasks becoming urgent. For example, if you do a lot of troubleshooting on your project. Spend time fixing errors beforehand to decrease the time cleaning up after the errors.

## 3) Urgent and Not Important

It is recommended not to spend time here either. Since the tasks are still not important and you're still not progressing towards your goals. However, these tasks are urgent, therefore you can't schedule them. They're also hard to ignore, since urgent action are often in your face and demand attention, e.g. a phone call or a colleague who interrupts.

You need to find a way to deal with these as quickly as possible. One way is to decrease the chance of other people disturbing you. You can do this by putting up a busy sign on your door. Next, if they get past the busy sign, you need to handle their interruptions quickly. Say up front that you're very busy and ask them to state their business quickly. There is no point in just sending them away, since they already succeeded in disturbing you. You might as well listen to their request and note it down. As soon as you know why they disturbed you, send them away to continue working on the important stuff.

## 4) Not Urgent and Not Important

You should not spend any time on activities in this quadrant. When is something not important? If it doesn't help you in any way to progress towards your goals, if it doesn't progress you toward your goals, then why should you spend time doing it?

When is something not urgent? If it doesn't matter when it is done, then it's not urgent. It can be done today, or it can be done next week or even next year, it doesn't matter.

The combination of not urgent and not important is the worst quadrant to spend your time in. No time should be wasted on anything that is *not urgent and not important'. So, it* should not be done at all, or it should be ignored, deleted or destroyed!

**Summary of the Eisenhower Method**

**Urgent and important**: Do these and when done, spend time thinking about how to avoid the situation in the future.

**Urgent and not important**: Avoid these as much as possible. When you're interrupted, handle it as fast as possible or delegate to your subordinate.

**Not urgent and important**: While action is not urgent, all your available time should go to this quadrant. You plan a date to do it before it becomes urgent.

**Not urgent and not important**: Don't do these, ignore them and start spending time in the *'not urgent and important'* zone.

You can make a goal of spending at least 80% of your time in the *'Not urgent and important'* quadrant. The other 20% will be divided between *'urgent and important'* and *'urgent and not important'*.

Always use the Eisenhower method when adding items to your to-do-list. Always ask yourself whether it is important and whether it is urgent. Bear in mind that doing 20% of the most important tasks will give 80% of the expected results.

## 5.4.2 Past, Present and Future

As human beings we exist in time. You and I are strongly influenced by the past, the present and our expectations of the future. As a leader you need to understand the influence of your past, manage the pressures of today and create a compelling vision of the future.

Time always comes in three stages: past, present and future. The past is the time that has come and gone forever. The present is the time you have now. What you do, you do it in the present time. The future is the time that will come. You better plan your future before it comes and becomes the present.

History is about the future. We study the past to learn about our present and how we can achieve the future we want, both as individuals and as a community. Donald Trump said: 'I try to learn from the past, but I plan for the future by focusing exclusively on the present. That's where the fun is.'

**The Pull of the past**

The past is gone we cannot do anything about it now, but we are capable of shaping our present and our future. However, people have to know about their past. The knowledge of their history gives them knowledge and power to shape the future.

**The Formula for Accelerated Change**

The past is gone, we keep lessons to better shape the present and predict the future. The present is the time in which you can be proactive about the future; so you don't have to be reactive.

We exist and live in the present. But we have a history – a personal past – that influences how we see the world. As people we hold tightly to the habits and beliefs of our past. And as leaders we become emotionally invested in our past successes. The beliefs and habits that underpinned our past success become deeply embedded in our leadership approach and style.

It's human nature to see the present through the lens of the past. However, this tendency causes us to use what worked yesterday in an attempt to solve tomorrow's problems. Even when all the facts are to the contrary, we tend to act and behave according to beliefs and principles from our past. When our past beliefs are strongly held they prevent us from embracing the new.

Leaders whose vision is limited by their past experiences become rapidly irrelevant in a rapidly changing world. Failure begins when we deny, ignore or rationalise the rapidly changing reality. Instead we focus on protecting the status quo, investing in what worked yesterday. When this happens, we become enslaved by the past. We fail to see how our past practices have become less and less effective. Instead of adopting new mindsets, practices and beliefs, we continue to rely on what worked in the past.

Your past and your history are useful if used as a springboard into the future. Not an excuse to retain the status quo. Visionary leaders selectively hold onto elements of the past, whilst they focus on investing in building for the future.

**What the great leaders say about the Past:**

'Yesterday's the past, tomorrow's the future, but today is a gift. That's why it's called the present.'
Bil Keane

'Yesterday is gone. Tomorrow has not yet come. We have only today. Let us begin.'
Mother Teresa

'Real generosity towards the future lies in giving all to the present.' Albert Camus

'The past is a ghost, the future a dream and all we ever have is now.' Bill Cosby

'One cannot and must not try to erase the past merely because it does not fit the present.'
Golda Meir

'A people without the knowledge of their past history, origin and culture is like a tree without roots.'
Marcus Garvey

## The Formula for Accelerated Change

> 'The only difference between the saint and the sinner is that every saint has a past, and every sinner has a future.' Oscar Wilde
>
> 'In this bright future you can't forget your past.' Bob Marley
>
> 'I like the dreams of the future better than the history of the past.' Thomas Jefferson
>
> 'History is the version of past events that people have decided to agree upon.' Napoleon Bonaparte
>
> 'We are made wise not by the recollection of our past, but by the responsibility for our future.' George Bernard Shaw
>
> 'A revolution is a struggle to the death between the future and the past.' Fidel Castro

### The Grip of the Present

When the present dominates, leaders become focused on the short-term. The emphasis is shifted to focus on rapid short-term results. When a leader's attention is on the short-term, the result is a focus on tactical initiatives, quick-fixes, silver bullets and reactive fire-fighting. This is the nature of the tactical and reactive management focus in many organisations today. All this comes at the expense of investing in long-term vision and capability building. The focus is on the management of short-term results, rather than exercising leadership to build new sources of value and a compelling future vision.

### What the great leaders say about the Present:

> 'The past has no power over the present moment.' Eckhart Tolle
>
> 'Reflect upon your present blessings of which every man has many – not on your past misfortunes, of which all men have some.' Charles Dickens
>
> 'If we open a quarrel between past and present, we shall find that we have lost the future.' Winston Churchill
>
> 'Do not dwell in the past, do not dream of the future, concentrate the mind on the present moment.' Buddha

**The Formula for Accelerated Change**

## The Power of the Future

People tend to have a short-term focus. However, visionary leaders choose to invest in a compelling long-term vision.

Whilst concerns of the present often tend to dominate, short-term concerns must be considered within the context of a long-term future vision. The decisions and actions of the present are best viewed as a pathway to the future. Visionary leaders think beyond the outcomes of today. They're always thinking about 'what's next?'

In the same way, visionary leaders selectively leverage their past as a platform for the future. In so doing, they shorten the distance between today and their future vision. They do this by challenging the status quo – especially traditional thinking, habits and ideas about what does and does not work – best practices and commonly accepted wisdom.

The challenge for visionary leaders then is to create a balance between the present – short-term pressures – and the long-term future vision; to acknowledge the past whilst creating a compelling vision of the future. Not an easy task, but of critical importance if people are to succeed and thrive.

**What the great leaders say about the Future:**

'The future depends on what you do today.' Mahatma Gandhi

'The best way to predict the future is to create it.' Peter Drucker

'Change is the law of life. And those who look only to the past or present are certain to miss the future.' John F. Kennedy

'The future belongs to those who prepare for it today.' Malcolm X

'Prejudice is a burden that confuses the past, threatens the future and renders the present inaccessible.' Maya Angelou

'Real generosity toward the future lies in giving all to the present.' Albert Camus

'Losers live in the past. Winners learn from the past and enjoy working in the present toward the future.' Denis Waitley

'The best thing about the future is that it comes one day at a time.' Abraham Lincoln

## The Formula for Accelerated Change

'The future rewards those who press on. I don't have time to feel sorry for myself. I don't have time to complain. I'm going to press on.' Barack Obama

'If you think in terms of a year, plant a seed; if in terms of ten years, plant trees; if in terms of 100 years, teach the people.' Confucius

'The future starts today, not tomorrow.' Pope John Paul II

# VI. PARADIGM SHIFTS AND THE COLLAPSE OF MYTHS

The Formula for Accelerated Change allows you to think, understand and see things differently. It produces paradigm shifts and dismantles myths and traditions. It creates a radical change in thinking from an ordinary point of view to a new belief. The new belief helps you to redefine yourself and to find out who you really are. You realise that you have inner potential to achieve your dreams and to help other people make positive changes in their lives. You see things not as they are but as they should be. You find out that you are not who you are now but who you should be and created to become. Together with others with a common vision you can initiate actions together and make change that you could never have imagined.

## 6.1 Every human being is born to be a leader

Every human being is unique and original. Your face, your fingerprints and your DNA are unique and nobody else on earth has the same traits. You have no duplicate. As you have unique physical and biological traits, God has created you and assigned you a unique purpose and a mission to make a difference and an impact on earth. He has also equipped you with unique capabilities, talents and gifts to accomplish that purpose. The most important thing in your life is to discover your purpose and your given potential. The discovery of your life purpose gives you a vision to accomplish. To translate this vision into reality requires the leadership within you to be developed.

The most important thing to know in life is that you are born a potential leader. But to become a leader you have to develop the leadership potential trapped in you. Leading people is serving other people with the gifts or talents you have to make them better. As taught by Dr Myles Munroe: 'True leadership has less to do with ruling people and more to do with serving people'. So, to lead is to serve

For so long, leadership has been seen mainly as a political, business, religious or institutional trait where it has been confused with top positions. Leaders have been considered to be individuals occupying the top levels in the hierarchy, and other people on the lower rungs of the ladder or subordinates have been defined and seen as followers, and sometimes even as subjects. This is wrong. The truth is that leadership can be developed and found at any level or position of the hierarchy, from the lowest level to the top.

Throughout history, the people who made great changes were ordinary people who did extraordinary things. They did it by being driven by their vision. In the pursuit of their vision, they influenced others who followed their vision. This is how other people have seen them as leaders and history remembers them as such.

A paradigm shift happens when a person discovers his/her life purpose, creates his/her vision and develops an independent will and commitment to accomplish it.

If you do not see yourself as a leader, it is time to do some soul searching and discover your life purpose, your talent and your leadership niche. It is time to find out what change you are called to make in this world. When you have discovered these things, nobody, not even you will stop you. This is what happens to people like Mahatma Gandhi, Martin Luther King, Jr., Steve Jobs, etc. Like these giants, you have been created to make a difference on earth. No matter how small you think you are, you can become a giant in your area of leadership and impact the world. They did extraordinary things. They did it by being driven by their vision. In the pursuit of their vision, they influenced others who followed their vision. This is how other people have seen them as leaders and history remembers them as such. Visionary people lead change.

## 6.2 Visionary people in synergy have a nuclear power

Nuclear power is derived from energy that is released when relatively large atoms are split in a series of controlled nuclear reactions. The process of splitting an atom is known as nuclear fission.

Although they are tiny, atoms have a large amount of energy holding their nuclei together. Certain isotopes of some elements can be split and will release part of their energy as heat. This splitting is called fission. Uranium-235 (U-235) is one of the isotopes that fissions easily. During fission, U-235 atoms absorb loose neutrons. This causes U-235 to become unstable and split into two light atoms called fission products and release three neutrons that will hit other atoms and so on.

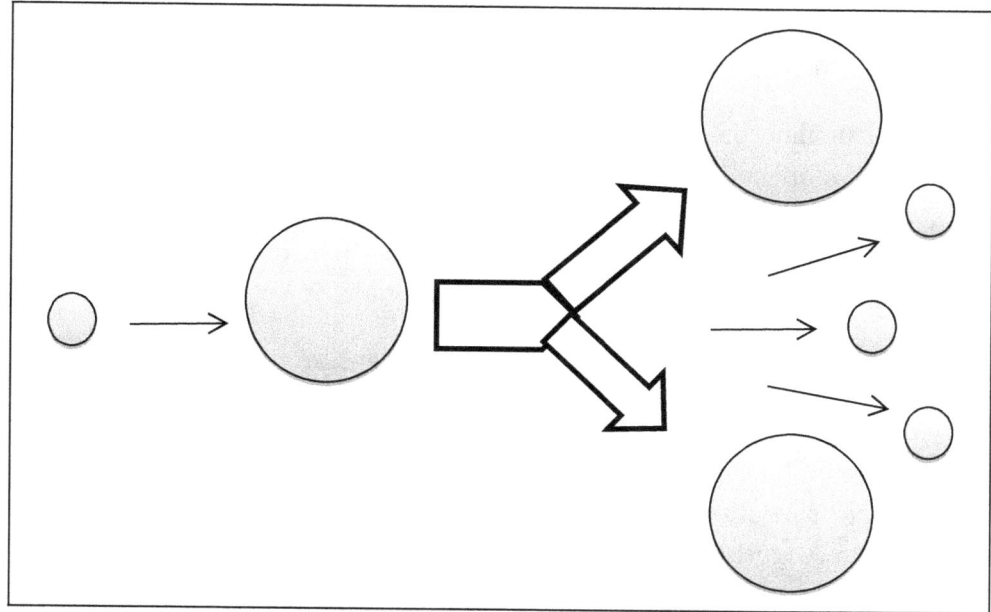

Figure 3: Nuclear fission

The combined mass of the fission products is less than that of the original U-235. The reduction occurs because some of the matter changes into energy. The energy is released as heat.

A series of fissions is called a chain reaction. If enough uranium is brought together under the right conditions, a continuous chain reaction occurs. This is called a self-sustaining chain reaction. A self-sustaining chain reaction creates a great deal of heat, which can be used to help generate electricity.

The fission process is caused by neutrons in the reactor core and both liberate considerable energy and produce more neutrons. The energy released is 1 million watt-days per gram of U-235 that undergoes fission, equivalent to 2.5 million times the energy released in burning one gram of coal. The produced neutrons can in turn yield additional fission events, producing a chain reaction that sustains energy production.

With a complete combustion or fission, approx. 8 kWh of heat can be generated from 1 kg of coal, approx. 12 kWh from 1 kg of mineral oil and around 24,000,000 kWh from 1 kg of uranium-235. Related to one kilogram, uranium-235 contains two to three million times the energy equivalent of oil or coal.

A **nuclear chain reaction** occurs when one single nuclear reaction causes an average of one or more subsequent nuclear reactions, thus leading to the possibility of a self-propagating series of these

### The Formula for Accelerated Change

reactions. Nuclear Chain Reactions are a simple, fast, yet powerful method which to produce both constructive and destructive forces.

You can actually calculate the amount of energy produced during a nuclear reaction with a fairly simple equation developed by Einstein: $E = mc^2$. In this equation, $E$ is the amount of energy produced, $m$ is the 'missing' mass, or the mass defect, and $c$ is the speed of light, which is a rather large number. The speed of light is squared, making that part of the equation a *very* large number that, even when multiplied by a small amount of mass, yields a *large* amount of energy.

The minimum amount of fissionable material needed to ensure that a chain reaction occurs is called the *critical mass*. Anything less than this amount is called *subcritical*.

Because of the tremendous amount of energy released in a fission chain reaction, the military implications of nuclear reactions were immediately realised. The first atomic bomb was dropped on Hiroshima, Japan, on August 6, 1945.

By analysing major changes that have taken place in the world, we realise that a vision acts a neutron and people behaves as atoms in a nuclear reaction. The first person whose mind is hit by a vision generates energy in the form of independent will, motivation and commitment to influence others. This person will transfer their vision to other people in the same way the produced neutrons hit the next atoms. By taking on the vision, these people will start to influence other people and so on. This is how a chain reaction is produced among people.

There are many examples that demonstrate this analogy such as the development of Christianity during the last 2000 years and the recent development of social media such as Facebook, Twitter, etc. Their followers' growth graphs follow the same pattern of the Formula for Accelerated Change. As calculated in Appendix 1, a graph of the Formula for Accelerated Change is generated here below:

**The Formula for Accelerated Change**

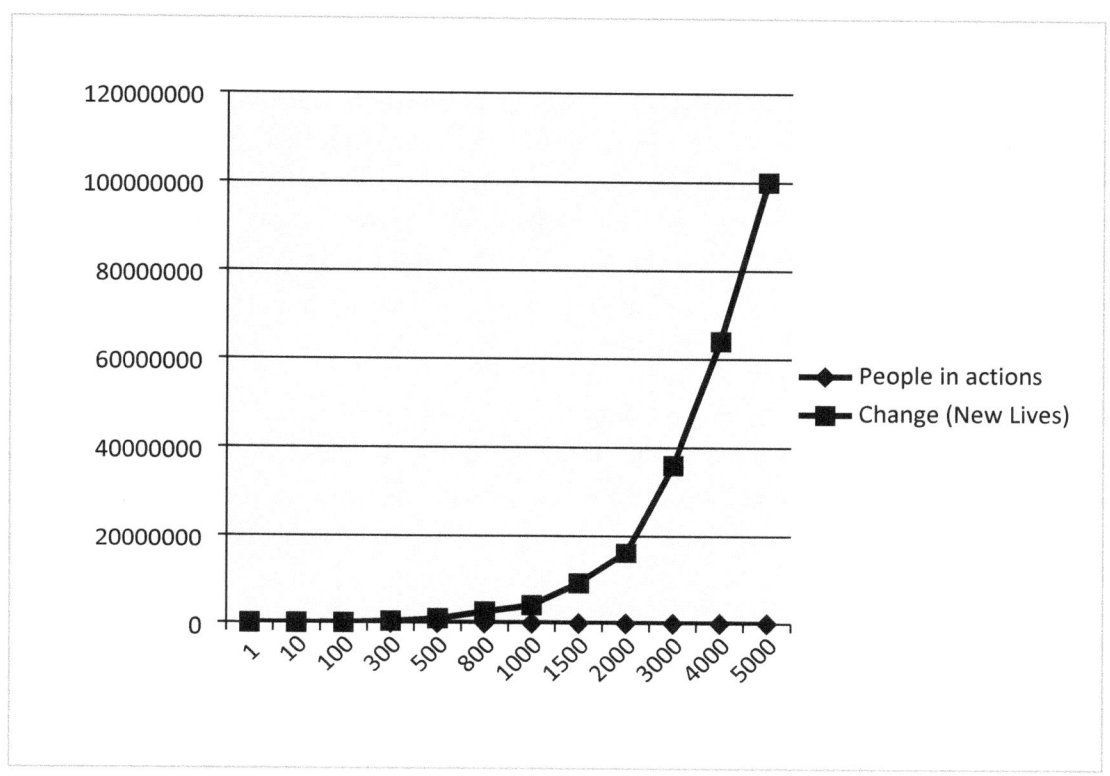

Figure 4: Formula for Accelerated Change – producing change (new lives)

## 6.3 The supremacy of a vision over the tyranny of a majority

The Formula for Accelerated Change allows predicting changes and their impact in a changing world. A vision is the key element that guides the desired change. A powerful vision ultimately creates changes in different areas at the same time. Nowadays with globalisation and social media technologies, a vision has no boundaries. A vision initiated by one individual in one place of the world can reach the whole world in a very short time inspiring many people to global actions. A powerful vision dismantles all walls and crosses borders. In fact, a powerful vision creates a new identity which is not based on the old characteristics of race, nationalities, regions, ideologies, religions, etc. For example, many people from all over the world with the same vision, ideas and interests are joining Facebook groups. These groups are creating new identities that produce global changes.

Until now democracy has been seen as majority rule. The majority rule is a 'doctrine by which a numerical *majority* of an organized group holds the power to make decisions binding on all in the group'. The majority is a higher number of people with something in common. Unfortunately, in many nations, communities or societies that commonality has been mainly based on culture, race, religion, ideology or beliefs.

Majority and minority are defined by numbers. Many democratic systems suggest that the people's majority is always right and has the right to lead everybody including those in the minority. This understanding of democracy creates 'the tyranny of the majority'. However, history has shown that the majority is not always right and the minority is not always wrong. In reality, the truth can be held by any individual, any minority or any majority. The truth remains the truth no matter where it comes from. As Mahatma Gandhi has put it: 'In the matter of conscience, the law of the majority has no place'.

The purpose of humankind is change. Everybody wants a better tomorrow than today. The desired change is guided by a vision of how things should be. The vision is created by the discovery of an unknown truth by an individual. When the visionary individual shares their vision with other persons who adopt it, it becomes a common vision for a group of people.

The vision generates the need and motivation for change and builds leadership that makes change in improving people's lives. The most important thing is the results or impact of change on people; less important is the number of people who have driven that change. The biggest historical changes known have been driven by individuals or small groups guided by a vision to shake the status quo supported by the majority. Many historical cases have proved the power of a personal vision over the minds of the majority.

**The Formula for Accelerated Change**

For change to happen, the most important and powerful element is the vision that destroys the perception and the weight of the majority and dismantles the status quo.

In the Formula for Accelerated Change, a vision has an exponential effect on people. An interesting note about change is that there are typically two types of people present in any change: those who lead and those who follow at a given time. You only need to create a common vision and build a critical mass of people to induce change in a group, a community, a nation or in the whole world.

Empirically observed, the critical mass is more or less equal to the square root of the total number of people to be impacted by the desired change. As a result, change happens when a small number of people with a common vision leads or influences a big number of people to have the desired change. For example, 10 people with a common vision can influence and make change among 100 people. In the same way, 1,000 people with a common vision will lead at least 1,000,000 followers.

Ultimately, a vision outruns the number of people and creates a new situation of 'the supremacy of vision' over the 'tyranny of majority' or 'tyranny of numbers'.

The vision provides diversity and unity among people. It creates a new identity that crosses all borders and cultures. The bottom line is 'the vision creates a new majority'.

If you want to make change in a community, in a society or a country, just have a vision and share your vision with the critical mass of people you want to impact and the desired change will inevitably happen through influence. This is how the great leaders have changed the world.

## 6.4 Change is from a vision, not from an individual

Vision always ignites change because it does not allow settling with the status quo. A visionary leader always seeks to attain their vision. A vision is like a guiding star and it is not reached as a destination in a limited time. As you get near it, it still seems to be far away. A vision is a picture of an ideal and perfect situation people want to be in or see happen. Visionary people always take actions and work to make change in order to get closer to their vision quickly. For a visionary leader time is too short and each day counts until the last day. A ready visionary is always in hurry. They are busy every day with lots of things to do and move forward. An individual lifetime span is too short for a vision to be achieved. A vision crosses generations. A vision is passed on from generation to generation. Looking back in history, great leaders never reached their visions, they passed it on to other generations; and even now their visions live on. However, visionary leaders fix goals, objectives and missions to be achieved in a given time. They initiate and carry out concrete actions to achieve specific objectives, goals and missions. Every time some goals are attained, new ones get fixed to pursue the journey towards the vision.

### The Formula for Accelerated Change

Jesus Christ had a vision for the Kingdom of God, and He worked hard during His last three years on earth and passed His work on to His disciples. His vision was transferred to Christian leaders from generation to generation until now. Jesus Christ accomplished his mission on earth to redeem humanity but yet all not all the people are yet saved. The work goes on. His vision is still to be reached.

Martin Luther King, Jr. had a dream. His dream or vision was to make the United States of America a country with equal rights and opportunities for all its citizens, including African-Americans. He reached some goals to abolish racial discrimination in many areas including public transportation, employment, voting, and education. Despite great developments made, the USA is still struggling to attain King's dream. The dream of equality regardless of race is still far away; cases of discrimination against African-Americans are still common.

Nelson Mandela struggled to abolish discrimination in South Africa and allow all South Africans to benefit from the wealth of their country. However, he succeeded in making South Africa a democratic state with equal voting rights for all. After his death, his successors are still working hard to get closer to Mandela's vision. The social and economic divide is still wide. The poverty among the majority of South Africans limits opportunities for inclusive prosperity.

In the corporate world, business people have visions for which they always bring innovations of new business models and technologies to make changes. The late Steve Jobs was a technological champion and businessman in the last decades of the 20th Century. Steve Jobs' mission statement for Apple in 1980 was: 'To make a contribution to the world by making tools for the mind that advance humankind.' Steve Jobs died in 2011 and Apple still works on digital tools to improve humankind.

In all walks of life, personal, social, economic, cultural, technological arenas, visions are started but never reached. Achieving a vision is a continuous and a never ending process. Visionary leaders work hard during their lifetime to get closer to their visions, but the time will come to pass it on to their successors; but their visions will live on. During their lifetime genuine visionary leaders keep leading. Visionary leaders pursue their dreams until they die.

A visionary leader does not get a job, he gets a mission to accomplish and a situation to move closer to the fixed vision. There is often confusion between a leadership position and a high-level official title or office. Being a president, minister, CEO, bishop, director or chief does not automatically qualify a person as a leader. A person with an official title or position can be a good manager but not necessarily a good leader. A visionary leader is a person who pursues a vision without being mandated or employed for it. A visionary leader does not need a title or a position. With or without a title or position, a visionary leader will work and struggle continuously to achieve the vision. A visionary leader never becomes complacent. A visionary leader always generates new ideas to challenge the status quo. Visionary leaders keep inspiring changes right up to their death. Unlike an official title or position that has a mandate and a term limit, visionary leaders do not need a mandate and have no term limit; they never relinquish their leadership position. Visionary leaders with official titles or positions would relinquish their job but never their work of making change. They continue leading on ideas (not on people) that seek changes. However, because visionary leaders are always aware of the fact that their life will be shorter than their vision, they will strive to mentor and empower other people who will assume the mantle of their vision when they are no longer there. The priority of visionary leaders is to ensure that even in their absence the vision will live on. The activity of empowering, training and mentoring new leaders becomes a top priority for a visionary leader. The vision is more important than the visionary. A visionary dies but the vision lives on and produces change endlessly. The vision is the eternal legacy of a visionary leader, and the success of any leader is determined by the success of their successors in fulfilling the vision.

## 6.5 You have sufficient resources to achieve your success

People have been made to believe that poverty is linked to material and financial resources. It is assumed that you are rich if you have abundant material and financial resources or you are poor if you have none or not enough to meet all your needs. People see lack of financial and material means as a limiting factor to achieving progress and success. This understanding has created a mindset of poverty and a mentality that has trapped many people in poverty.

That fact that you do not have a house, a car, a loaded bank account or a full wardrobe should not mean that you are poor. Perhaps now you are lacking some material things but it does not mean that you do not have the capability to get them any time. The most important thing is to know what you need, why you need them and how you could get them if you really need them. The truth is that if you really need them you will get them no matter what. To get what you want will depend on how you use what you have now and how to tap into your internal potential and seize opportunities that are around you.

It is important and urgent to realise that what you have now is sufficient to get what you need. You can start with the resources you have to achieve development, progress and success you want. God has built in you the capacity to succeed and has surrounded you with the resources you need to achieve that. First start by giving value and managing well what you have; second build on what you have to achieve your vision and make the change you want.

The key to your success is having a vision and a life purpose. According to the Formula for Accelerated Change, your vision will change you by creating your self-worth and building your capacity to achieve. This new mindset will dismantle the poverty mentality and consequently you will discover valuable gifts you have to offer to the world. Once you realise the potential you have and how you can offer your gifts and serve others, then all the human, material and financial resources you need will come to you. This is how you will find everything you need and become successful.

Nobody was born to be poor, but unfortunately many people have developed a poverty mentality that keeps them poor. They do not realise how rich they are and miss the opportunity to use the abundant resources endowed on them to develop, progress and succeed. What people need to overcome poverty is to have a vision, a new mindset and visionary leadership to make change happen. There is an urgent need for leaders who are able to inspire a collective vision, mobilise people around strategic actions for social and economic transformation.

## 6.6 Education systems are wrong and should change

Everybody has been created and equipped by God with the potential to grow and succeed in life. Every born child is predestined for a successful in life. The education of children, youth and adult people is supposed to contribute to the growth and development of individuals to attain their full potential. Unfortunately, many people fail to live abundant and successful lives. The reasons why people fail do not necessarily come from within individuals but from external environments and education systems created by people. Mostly people's failures are embedded in the ineffective education systems that fail to equip them with sufficient knowledge, skills and attitude to realise their full potential. An education system fails when it does not help people to know their life purpose and leaves them with confused and broken lives characterised by unhappiness, poverty, unemployment, conflicts, etc. This unfortunate situation of poor and unfulfilled lives unfortunately remains common in many countries, particularly in Africa as a result of inappropriate education systems. Now, the big question is to know what is wrong with the education systems in many countries.

The Formula for Accelerated Change helps us to do an analysis of education systems and respond to the above question. It allows us to evaluate their relevance and effectiveness. The formula tells us that there is no success without a vision. So, the most important thing is to know if the current education systems allow young generations to create a positive vision and discover their life purpose. Let us find out by asking some university students what they intend to achieve with their lives at the end of their studies. Their answers to this question could be very surprising. Most of them would respond that they do not know or they have not thought about it yet. These students are in the same situation as someone who starts walking or driving without knowing the destination; and in the middle of the road he/she is asked by someone else where he/she is going and he/she responds

**The Formula for Accelerated Change**

that he/she does not know or he/she has not figured it out yet. It seems crazy to start a journey without knowing where you are going. Life is like a journey, so it is very important to know the destination. The life destination is given by a personal vision and a life purpose to accomplish. Students should know why they are studying and what they want to achieve and become in life. If they know the WHY, it be would easier to choose the WHAT to study and commit to it. So, each student should know first his/her vision and life purpose as source of motivation do study. The objective of an education system should be to allow students to have a vision, a life purpose, and give them the knowledge and skills to achieve it.

The current education systems are pushing young people to focus on getting jobs after their studies for the sake of earning money and a living. Unfortunately, paid jobs have become scarce and many graduates remain unemployed, disoriented, confused about their uncertain future. The education systems are designed to produce job seekers instead of job creators, people who initiate work to achieve purpose. To create and innovate requires having a vision and an independent will to solve problems and make a change that will benefit others.

The problem of unemployment among youth is deep rooted in that ineffective education systems do not orient young people to their vision. Most young people choose to study courses that are too easy to do and that are likely to have more job opportunities; this is why in some areas there are too many qualified applicants and in other areas there is a lack of qualified people. You see this in where there are too many qualified people in social sciences and management and less in technical and engineering fields. This situation creates an imbalance on the job market with negative consequences on the economic development of countries. How could you have more accountants and managers than technicians and engineers? Without technicians and engineers to produce commodities, what will managers be managing?

The education system of a country should be based on a national vision and the personal visions of its citizen, especially of its young people. All education programmes and curricula should first enable students to discover their vision and life purpose and show them how they will realise them and contribute to the national vision.

Another issue raised from the analysis of many education systems is related to methods of teaching. The ultimate goal of teaching is to make positive changes by improving knowledge, skills and attitudes in people. Teaching should not only focus on personal change but also on societal transformation. According to the Formula for Accelerated Change, change happens in a society when people work and act in synergy, this means that people have to complete each other instead of competing against each other. By looking carefully at the teaching methods, the findings show that students are encouraged to compete against each other by working individually instead of supporting

**The Formula for Accelerated Change**

team works and synergy. In a workplace people do not work in isolation, that is why the teaching methods should emulate the workplace environment by encouraging students to work together to create, innovate and solve problems. This is why there should be less individual tests or exams and more projects in teams where students work together to solve problems. Fostering the culture of working in synergy is necessary for accelerated and sustainable change as it produces exponential impact over time. That is why students should work in teams of people to get 'P² effect' of the formula. It is this effect that accelerates change.

Another big problem found in the education systems is the building of uniformity and conformity that push students to think alike. A human being is unique and people are diverse. Individuals have different talents and gifts, and that is why complementarity is essential to build synergy. The current teaching methods want students to be identical and think the same way; this is why tests and exams have the same questions with an expectation to have the same answers. Students are given texts and formula to memorise and regurgitate in tests and exams. These teaching methods do not encourage critical thinking, imagination, creativity and innovation. No wonder then that the most legendary genii and entrepreneurs are school dropouts, i.e. Thomas Edison, Albert Einstein, Bill Gates, Steve Jobs, Mark Zuckerberg, etc.

---

**How Einstein Quit School**

In his youth, Albert Einstein attended a traditional school in Munich, Germany, just like many other children of his time. He received good grades and was particularly accomplished in the field of mathematics.

However, he absolutely detested school because he could not stand the way the teachers taught. He thought that everything was far too objective, there was no room for questioning or thought, with the classes instead focusing on strict memorisation.

Einstein wanted to be free to express his own thoughts, and to pursue the specific subjects in which he was interested. Einstein found it very difficult to do that in such a rigid educational environment.

When he was 15, his teacher suggested that he leave school, and he took the suggestion and did not return.

---

In conclusion, the education systems should have a purpose of developing people's talents and gifts, creating a vision and acting in order to improve lives and create a better world. Teaching methods, courses, programmes and curricula should not only provide knowledge but should also provide practical skills, positive attitudes and new mindsets. They should be built on diversity and the

**The Formula for Accelerated Change**

specific talents of the individual. From the perspective of the Formula for Accelerated Change, the teaching methods and contents should focus on helping people to:

1. discover purpose and create a vision;
2. develop leadership skills;
3. develop imagination, creativity and innovation;
4. improve knowledge, entrepreneurship and problem-solving skills;
5. team and synergy building;
6. plan, implement actions effectively and efficiently;
7. manage time properly and act proactively.

## 6.7 You are an agent of change

An agent of change initiates a desired change. God has created you with a purpose to fulfil on earth, so you have to live a purpose-driven life. What you need now is to discover your purpose and create a vision of a change you want to happen. If you don't initiate change somebody else will do it and that person will control you. In this case you become a victim or a subject who will be reactive to what is happening to you. Instead of becoming reactive, it is time for you to become proactive and initiate the change you desire. This is the only way to control you own life and influence others positively.

To become a change agent, you start by making change in yourself before you seek change for other people. Changing yourself will transform you into a leader who will influence others and the society you live in. From personal change, you can make change in a group, an organisation, a corporate, a community, a county, and in the whole world. The world is waiting for you to make it a better place to live in.

In reference to the Formula for Accelerated Change, there are four things you need to do to make change quickly at any level:

1) have a **vision** of the situation you want;
2) identify a critical mass of **people** you want to impact and influence them with your visions;
3) plan **actions**; and implement them
4) to change the status quo and produce **change** over **time**.

In Appendix 1, you will find simple tools that will assist you to plan, have your road map of actions and realise the change you desire.

## 6.8 How development aid sustains poverty in Africa

The statement of saying that 'development aid sustains poverty in Africa' seems dangerous and cynical but a deep analysis of the development aid strategies applied in many development programmes confirms this reality. To understand the development aid reality in Africa, some questions have to be asked. Why do the majority of people in Africa remain in poverty after many decades of development aid programmes? Is there anything wrong with development aid in Africa? Is it because Africans do not want development or do not work enough to achieve results? Do people in Africa want to change? What is really wrong?

Let us try to understand the situation of development aid in Africa by using the Formula for Accelerated Change. This formula is based on four key factors and principles of improving lives of people, namely vision, people, actions and time. Analysing development aid approaches and strategies in Africa by using the formula we find out why they have failed to uproot poverty.

In the last two decades development aid has been guided by the 'poverty reduction strategies' and Millennium Development Goals (MDGs) that so far have not produced the expected results. According to the Formula for Accelerated Change, positive change starts with a vision. Without a vision people fail (perish). So, the key question is to know what kind of vision has been fixed for development aid strategies, such as poverty reduction strategies and MDGs in Africa. What is the vision for Africa? Is it a vision with a bright future or a gloomy future? It is clear that seeing a bright future motivates people but a gloomy future discourages and condemns people and does not call for positive actions. So, what picture of the future do we get from these development aid strategies?

Many development aid strategies in Africa are based on the concept of 'poverty reduction'. The question here is to find out why is the verb 'reduce' used instead of 'eradicate'? Why is the focus on poverty? Why is the concept of 'poverty reduction' used? Why not the concept of 'wealth creation' or 'increasing prosperity'? The two concepts paint two different pictures of the future. The first one gives a negative vision of 'sustainable poverty'; it is saying that poverty can only be reduced and people have to live with a certain degree of poverty forever. However, the second concept gives a positive vision, it allows people to understand that they have the potential to create wealth and become prosperous. The poverty reduction concept comes from a pessimist paradigm that sees poverty, ignorance, chaos, disease and insecurity as Africa's destiny. This thinking promotes poverty reduction programmes designed and built on the premise of 'half empty' instead of opting for 'wealth creation' programmes built on the principle of 'half full'. There is no doubt that a positive vision gives positive results and a negative vision gives negative results. Having a negative vision is worse than having no vision at all.

**The Formula for Accelerated Change**

Another key factor of change is people. Change and development are about people. Change starts with people. Change is made by people themselves, first by changing themselves and then changing others. Once people have a common vision and are sufficiently equipped to take actions, they make the change they want. However, the analysis of development aid strategies built on the 'poverty' concept shows that priority has not been put on empowering people, but on activities and results related to production, infrastructures, institutions, etc. The impact of these activities, which are not 'people centred', cannot become sustainable without empowering people. People have to improve their knowledge, skills and attitude to maintain and expand and roll out the outcomes of development programmes. Unfortunately, in the last five decades, the development aid strategies in Africa have been built on a negative vision of poverty, and have not focused on empowerment of people as a priority.

Now it is high time to change and come up with development strategies and approaches built on a positive vision that gives priority to the empowerment of people in all actions undertaken. It is imperative for a country to have a national vision that guides policies, sectoral strategies, programmes and projects. The same requirement is valid for communities, organisations, public and private institutions. The starting point of change and development is the creation of a clear and positive vision, building the capacity of people to have a common vision and ownership of their destiny.

Considering the concepts developed from the Formula for Accelerated Change, the development strategies have to be based on a '**vision approach**'. The vision approach is where all development strategies, programmes and projects are built on a vision. A vision owned and shared by people creates synergy, motivates them to action, accelerates change and produce exponential impact.

The vision approach introduces the new design of development programme/project planning and implementation tools. Among other key tools to redesign is the 'Logical Framework', where vision becomes the first element of the project description. As well the Objectively Verifiable Indicators (OVIs) will have to focus more on measuring improvement in people's lives and how they are creating wealth and becoming prosperous.

**The Formula for Accelerated Change**

**New Logical Framework with a 'vision approach'**

| Project Description | | Objectively Verifiable Indicators (OVIs) | Means of Verification | Assumptions and Risks |
|---|---|---|---|---|
| Vision | What picture of the future do we want? | How will we know we've been successful (vision is being achieved)? | How will we check our reported results? | What assumptions underlie the structure of our project and what is the risk they will not prevail? |
| Purpose | Why are we doing this? | Same as above | Same as above | Same as above |
| Goals | What results do we expect? | Same as above | Same as above | Same as above |
| Outputs | What are the deliverables? | Same as above | Same as above | Same as above |
| Activities | What are we doing? | Inputs | Costs | |
| | | | | Conditions |

### 6.9 Applying 'a vision approach' in achieving Sustainable Development Goals (SDGs)

The successor to the 8 Millennium Development Goals (MDGs), the new set of 17 Sustainable Development Goals (SDGs) – adopted at a global summit of heads of state and government in New York from September 25 to 28, 2015, is essentially an agreed 'Global Vision' that will guide people of the planet on a sustainable path to a better world by 2030. It will form the bedrock of a new development agenda that spells out how people can work together to promote dignity, equality, justice, shared prosperity and well-being for all, while protecting the environment for future generations.

The success of the SDGs will require the participation of all people on the planet. People together in their respective countries, counties, districts, communities, groups, families, institutions, companies, etc. will have to own that global vision by localising and adapting the SDGs to their contexts, areas of intervention and specific needs. That is why all countries as well as institutions, communities, groups, families and individuals need to own and incorporate the SDGs targets into their respective development agendas. All development goals and targets have to be set so as to build synergies, achieve inclusive and people-centred development that promote shared prosperity that leaves no one behind. All individuals will have to play their respective roles, get actively involved and own the process of transformation and shape their lives. The priority action of any development initiative would be to empower each individual to realise their potential, participate actively and contribute to

## The Formula for Accelerated Change

the common good. Sustainable development goals will be achieved when each person is engaged and everyone is working together to achieve common visions and build a better world.

Applying a vision approach and using the Formula for Accelerated Change in achieving SDGs consists of defining common visions that will guide the development plans, programmes, projects and activities at global, national, local, group, organisational, family and personal level that are consistent to the SDGs. From global to the personal level, visions, policies, strategies, plans, programmes, projects and activities have to be coherent and connected to the SDGs as presented in the table below.

| Level of Vision | Global visions | National visions | Local and Community visions | Organisational visions | Family and Personal visions |
|---|---|---|---|---|---|
| Entities or stakeholders | International organisations, multilateral agencies and multinational companies. | National governments, national agencies and companies. | Local authorities and agencies at region, province, county, district and community level. | Companies, NGOs, voluntary and faith organisations and groups. | Families and Individuals. |
| Instruments | Multinational plans and programmes, International agreements and protocols. | National policies, strategies, plans, programmes and projects. | Local development plans, programmes, projects and activities. | Business plans, strategic plans, action plans, programmes, projects and activities. | Family and Personal development plans, projects and activities. |

**Sustainable Development Goals**

1. End poverty in all its forms everywhere.
2. End hunger, achieve food security and improved nutrition and promote sustainable agriculture.
3. Ensure healthy lives and promote well-being for all at all ages.
4. Ensure inclusive and equitable quality education and promote lifelong learning opportunities for all.
5. Achieve gender equality and empower all women and girls.
6. Ensure availability and sustainable management of water and sanitation for all.
7. Ensure access to affordable, reliable, sustainable and modern energy for all.
8. Promote sustained, inclusive and sustainable economic growth, full and productive employment and decent work for all.
9. Build resilient infrastructure, promote inclusive and sustainable industrialisation and foster innovation.
10. Reduce inequality within and among countries.
11. Make cities and human settlements inclusive, safe, resilient and sustainable.
12. Ensure sustainable consumption and production patterns.
13. Take urgent action to combat climate change and its impacts.
14. Conserve and sustainably use the oceans, seas and marine resources for sustainable development.

Juvenal TURATINZE

## The Formula for Accelerated Change

15. Protect, restore and promote sustainable use of terrestrial ecosystems, sustainably manage forests, combat desertification, and halt and reverse land degradation and halt biodiversity loss.
16. Promote peaceful and inclusive societies for sustainable development, provide access to justice for all and build effective, accountable and inclusive institutions at all levels.
17. Strengthen the means of implementation and revitalize the global partnership for sustainable development.

The achievement of SDGs requires a new brand of leaders, visionary leaders at global, national and local levels and in all areas targeted by SDGs. Only leaders with a new mindset will be able to mobilise and include everybody in the process and make change in the lives of the people. Empowering people to change, building synergies in them and organising collective actions to achieve visions from the local to the global levels is the best way to achieve SGDs and make the world a better place for all.

# APPENDIX 1: Tools of Change Planning

### Personal Change Planning Tool

| First mane: | | Family name: | |
|---|---|---|---|
| Birth date : | Age : … years | Life expectancy :… years (Years you hope to live) | Years left to live: …. years |

**Self-assessment:**

**Who Am I? (Define who you are in three words)**

| 1 | | 2 | | 3 | |
|---|---|---|---|---|---|

**My current assets**

| | Asset | Monetary Value |
|---|---|---|
| 1 | | |
| 2 | | |
| 3 | | |

**Achievements**

| | Life Dimension | Current level satisfaction (%) | Immediate action for improvement |
|---|---|---|---|
| 1 | Physical (health) | | |
| 2 | Intellectual (Degrees) | | |
| 3 | Professional (work) | | |
| 4 | Economic (income) | | |
| 5 | Emotional (love) | | |
| 6 | Social (Friendship) | | |
| 7 | Spiritual (Beliefs and values) | | |

**Vision – Mission – Life objectives - Actions:**

| | Immediate Action | In 5 years | In 10 years | In 20 years |
|---|---|---|---|---|
| Who do I want to become (Personality) | | | | |
| What do I want to do (Work, job, career) | | | | |
| What do I want to have (Assets) | | | | |
| What do I want to achieve in my society (impact on other people) | | | | |

# The Formula for Accelerated Change

**My Legacy (How you want to be remembered after your death):**

>  

**Name, Date and Signature:**

## Organisational Change Planning

### 1. Vision – Raison d'être

(Why does your organisation exist? What change does your organisation want to make in society?)

### 2. Mission

(What is your organisation going to do to achieve the vision?)

### 3. Leadership, structures, systems and procedures

(Determine leadership, structures, systems and procedures needed to achieve mission and vision)

### 4. Objectives

(Key goals fixed in time to achieve the mission)

### 5. Areas of interventions

(In which areas of life do you intervene? In which sectors do you want to make change?)

### 6. Targeted people

(People you want to impact and improve the lives of)

## The Formula for Accelerated Change

### 7. Strategies

(Approaches to take and use what you have and achieve what you want)

### 8. Activities

(Tangible actions to be carried out to achieve the objectives)

### 9. Human resources

(People needed to carry out actions)

### 10. Material resources

(Materials and equipment needed to get activities done)

### 11. Actions plan (schedule of activities)

|   | What to do? | Who is doing it? | When to do it? | Indicators of achievement |
|---|---|---|---|---|
| 1 | | | | |
| 2 | | | | |
| 3 | | | | |
| 4 | | | | |
| 5 | | | | |

# The Formula for Accelerated Change

## Enterprise or Company Change Planning

### 1. Vision – Raison d'être

(Why does your enterprise exist? What change does your enterprise want to make in society?)

### 2. Mission

(What is your enterprise going to do to achieve the vision?)

### 3. Leadership, structures, systems and procedures

(Determine leadership, structures, systems and procedures needed to achieve the mission and vision)

### 4. Objectives

(Key goals fixed in time to achieve the mission)

### 5. Products or services

(What products or services do you want to offer to the market?)

### 6. Customers

(Where is the demand? People you target with your products and services

### 7. Marketing Strategies

(Approaches to take to reach the market and get customers)

### 8. Activities

(Tangible actions to be carried out to sell your products or services)

## The Formula for Accelerated Change

### 9.  Human resources

(People to employ to carry out activities)

### 10. Material resources

(Materials and equipment you need to get activities done)

### 11. Actions plan (schedule of activities)

|   | What to do? | Who is doing it? | When to do it? | Indicators of achievement |
|---|---|---|---|---|
| 1 |   |   |   |   |
| 2 |   |   |   |   |
| 3 |   |   |   |   |
| 4 |   |   |   |   |
| 5 |   |   |   |   |

## The Formula for Accelerated Change

### A Community, Country or World Change Planning

#### 1. Vision – Raison d'être

(What life situation should your people have?)

#### 2. Mission

(What is going to be done collectively to achieve the vision?)

#### 3. General Objectives

(Key goals fixed in time to achieve the mission)

#### 4. Priority Areas of interventions

(In which priority areas of life do you want to make improvement? In which specific sectors do you want to make change?)

#### 5. Policies and Strategies

(Directions and approaches to take to use what you have and achieve what you want)

#### 6. Leadership, structures, systems and procedures

(Determine leadership, structures, systems and procedures needed to implement policies and strategies, achieve mission and vision)

#### 7. Plans, Programmes and Projects

(Plans, Programmes and projects define specific objectives, activities and target groups to achieve the general objectives)

Juvenal TURATINZE

**The Formula for Accelerated Change**

### 8. Human resources

(People needed to carry out actions)

### 9. Material resources

(Materials and equipment needed to get activities done)

### 10. Actions plan (schedule of activities)

|   | What to do? | Who is doing it? | When to do it? | Indicators of achievement |
|---|---|---|---|---|
| 1 |   |   |   |   |
| 2 |   |   |   |   |
| 3 |   |   |   |   |
| 4 |   |   |   |   |
| 5 |   |   |   |   |

# APPENDIX 2: Calculation of change using the Formula for Accelerated Change

**$V \times P^2 \times A \times T = C$ (Visionary People in Action over Time make Change)**

| Vision | Size | Value | Type of Vision |
|---|---|---|---|
| Small vision | V1 | 1 | Vision for an individual, a family, a group or an association, that targets less than 1000 people. |
| Average Vision | V2 | 2 | Vision: vision for a community, an institution, a corporate or a country, that targets between 1000 and 100 million people |
| Big and Global Vision | V3 | 3 | Vision for the world that targets more than 100 million of people. |

| Action | Size | Value | Type d'actions |
|---|---|---|---|
| First step actions | A1 | 1 | First strategic plan of actions |
| Second step actions | A2 | 2 | Second strategic plan of actions |
| Third step actions | A3 | 3 | Third strategic plan of actions |

| Time | Size | Value | Period |
|---|---|---|---|
| First time generation | T1 | 1 | 0 to 50 years |
| Second time generation | T2 | 2 | 50 to 100 years |
| Third time generation | T3 | 3 | From 100 years and beyond |

**Données de base**

| X= number of people | Y Value | Z Value |
|---|---|---|
| V - Vision | 1 | 2 |
| A - Actions | 1 | 2 |
| T - Time | 1 | 2 |

Juvenal TURATINZE

# The Formula for Accelerated Change

| X People in action | Y New lives (V1, A1, T1) | Z New lives (V2,A2, T2) |
|---:|---:|---:|
| 1 | 1 | 8 |
| 5 | 25 | 200 |
| 50 | 2,500 | 20,000 |
| 100 | 10,000 | 80,000 |
| 200 | 40,000 | 320,000 |
| 300 | 90,000 | 720,000 |
| 500 | 250,000 | 2,000,000 |
| 700 | 490,000 | 3,920,000 |
| 1000 | 1,000,000 | 8,000,000 |
| 1500 | 2,250,000 | 18,000,000 |
| 2000 | 4,000,000 | 32,000,000 |
| 2500 | 6,250,000 | 50,000,000 |

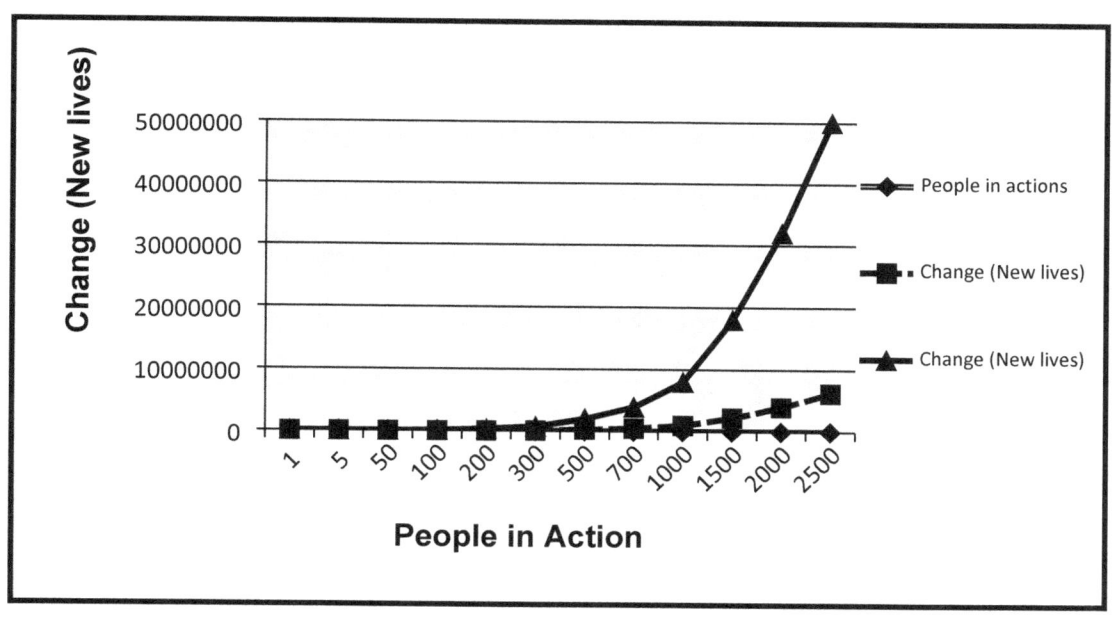

$$V_x P^2_x A_x T = C$$

**Visionary People together in Action over Time make Change**

It is difficult to predict or plan change accurately. Every day we face a challenge of making change we want or managing change to meet our desire. The Formula for Accelerated Change brings a solution to this problem. This formula enables you to plan change you want and make it happen quickly.

The Formula for Accelerated Change ($V_x P^2_x A_x T = C$) is translated as '**Visionary People together in Action over Time make Change**'; it is made by four key factors: **vision, people, actions** and **time**. Each factor is organic in its nature, because it grows with time when nourished with the right ingredients, such as purpose, leadership, action planning, time management, etc. These ingredients are developed to build the key factors of change. The combination of these factors produces the desired change. The produced change consists of 'improved lives'.

This book introduces a *Vision Approach* to change, success and sustainable development. It argues that every desired change starts with a vision. A vision gives a purpose to live for and ignites people to act. People working in synergy improve the lives of other people exponentially over time.

This book is guide for helping you to understand and develop the key factors of change (vision, people, actions and time) and ultimately will enable you to predict, plan and make the change you desire.

The Formula for Accelerated Change is your tool to become a visionary leader in an area of your talents. It will help you to realise paradigm shifts and dismantle myths around leadership, the rule of the majority, development and change. You will discover your potential and internal power to change yourself and the world around you. With a clear vision, you will serve others, achieve your purpose and leave an eternal legacy on earth.

Juvenal TURATINZE

## About the author

The author, **Juvenal Turatsinze**, holds a Bachelor's Degree in Agricultural and Food Engineering and a Master's Degree in Development Studies. He has more than 25 years of experience as a development worker and change agent. **He is an expert and consultant in Local Economic Development, Business Development and Sustainable Development.** His personal vision is a peaceful and better world without poverty where all human beings are able to use their potential to meet all their needs, live with dignity and serve others with their respective God-given gifts for the common good.